XAMNESIA

EVERYTHING I FORGOT IN MY SEARCH FOR AN UNREAL LIFE

LIZZIE HARWOOD

EDITOR DELUXE PRESS

Copyright © 2015 by Lizzie Harwood

All rights reserved.

No part of this book may be reproduced in any form or by any electronic or mechanical means, including information storage and retrieval systems, without written permission from the author, except for the use of brief quotations in a book review. Real names have been deleted or changed.

ISBN: 978-2955069004

Editor Deluxe Press

CONTENTS

Prologue	1
1. Invisibility 1	5
2. Men 1	13
3. Movement 1	19
4. Money 1	25
5. Myopia 1	35
6. Myopia 2	45
7. Invisibility 2	50
8. Mischief 1	60
9. Silence 1	71
10. Silence 2	78
11. Invisibility 3	83
12. Movement 2	92
13. Movement 3	99
14. Men 2	108
15. Mischief 2	115
16. Money 2	124
17. Crash 1	131
18. Men 3	140
19. Men 4	146
20. Silence 3	154
21. Movement 4	164
22. Mischief 3	169
23. Crash 2	176
24. Men 5	185
25. Movement 5	191
26. Invisibility 4	195
27. Movement 6	201
28. Men 6	211

29. Mischief 4	219
30. Invisibility 5	225
31. Crash 3	231
32. Men 7	240
33. Visibility 1	244
34. Love 1	250
35. Postscript	255
Acknowledgments	259
About the Author	261

PROLOGUE

On March 5, 2000, I wheel my bright-blue Samsonite through Gare du Nord station in Paris, clutching a ticket for the Eurostar to London Waterloo International. I have a seat in coach five because I smoke a pack a day. My shoulder bag bulges with toiletries and pajamas so I can stay overnight in London and go out with my buddy, Idora. My main preoccupation is where Idora and I will go that night (Notting Hill Arts Club, please).

Inside my case is one million in American dollars.

The money is in 100-dollar bills so it fills my suitcase two-thirds. Anyone X-raying my bag can't help but notice it's all cash. Before I shut it, a sea of Benjamin Franklins gaze with a look of disquiet at this unscheduled field trip. A thick, purple plastic band cossets each 10K wad.

In case you think I am part of some cult forced into money laundering, or like that woman from *Orange is the New Black*, I might mention that I volunteered for this.

That morning I got a safe cracker to open the hidden

wall safe in the property I manage because higher-ups requested that this cash get over to London today. I volunteered to take the cash because my overly adaptable personality reframes this illegal activity into 'doing what I have to do.' You know, like any other regular day in the office.

I roll toward the ticket barrier with nary a care.

No way do I pull myself aside with a stern, *"Lizzie, what are you doing?"*

This is because I believe I'm invisible and invincible… so smuggling undeclared cash over an international border, without so much as a letter to say whose money it is, poses no problem.

Steal the money?

Doesn't cross my mind.

There are several other trains further down the platform that could take me to Amsterdam, Hamburg, Cologne. I could be in Poland by sundown. I could easily abscond with all that cash in my suitcase, no sweat.

Nah, I keep right on rolling.

I clear check-in with a cigarette at my lips and an air of total indifference. Living in Paris yet barely speaking the language makes me a mime artist who smokes a lot, shrugs, and raises eyebrows to communicate.

I present my British passport to the double set of police in their tidy booths. The French police says nothing, the UK police bids me a good trip. I take that as 'good signs.' I'm on the right track. I hide my trusty passport with a sincere "Merci" and genuine "Thank you."

A sudden thought hits me: if Notting Hill Arts Club is

on the cards tonight, I really ought to grab a bottle of Veuve Clicquot at the kiosk after customs... to drink at Idora's place before going out. I can squeeze it into my Samsonite. The Benjamin Franklins can bunch up a little.

I am not panicked that I'll be grabbed or arrested. I believe I can slink around the whole world *unnoticed* if I choose because that's what has worked for me since I was a child.

I have a severe case of invisibility-plus-impulsive-behavior that I am calling, for the purposes of this memoir, *Xamnesia*.

It's a heady mix of feeling impervious to your reality. Like nothing can touch you. On March 5, 2000, I lived in an inner city fortress in Paris and had full-blown Xamnesia. No cure in sight.

I round the corner and sleepwalk right up to the customs agent with his muzzled, drug-sniffing Alsatian and ominous, gray X-ray machine. As if I were cloaked in a warm, gray fog.

What started me on the path to *this*—being twenty-seven and volunteering to smuggle cash from Paris to London? To see that I have to back way up—airplane-high—to see how *this* happened.

1

INVISIBILITY 1

I grew up in New Zealand in a quiet bay on an island that resembles the island on this book's cover.

It's where a lot of stuff started that led me to Xamnesia.

'The Barrier' as everyone calls Great Barrier Island, is an unpolished diamond in the Hauraki Gulf, fifty miles off Auckland. The east coast is peppered with surf beaches and shipwreck sites. The west coast is a string of mysterious coves. It's opossum-free and the inhabitants proudly use generators or windmills for power; driving beat-up Jeeps or Holdens on rough roads that only saw tarmac a decade ago.

Mom, when I talk about the Barrier, leaps on the topic with great fervor, reminding me of several murders that happened when we lived there that she personally *knows* who perpetrated what to whom.

And about the cult of personality going on in the north of the island where several women hung out making love to the leader and scribbling news of it on postcards to send to their parents back in the States.

And the dope growers, who were periodically busted and sent to Auckland prisons, laughing as they boarded the sea plane to incarceration because they had so much money in their post office bank accounts to return to.

And how my big sister Jocelyn's husband, Burke, pulled a knife on customers in the general store that my family owned and operated.

And how the one policeman said the island was a lifeboat you couldn't rock and that he was powerless to stop the tide of lawlessness running rampant.

But I have different memories of the Barrier.

Sure, I do remember my brother-in-law, Burke (twenty-one at the time), leaping atop a chest freezer and carving the air with a hunting knife because of some off-color remark from a customer. It may have been about Burke having sex with the man's wife, who knows? Burke had a lot going on, both in and out of his marriage to my sister.

I mainly remember all the fun we kids got up to because we lived a charmed, unsupervised life out in the bush, coming home to eat candy out of the boxes in the shop, refit ourselves with fresh flip-flops whenever we lost one, throw on our life jackets so we could go swimming in storms—nothing was ever a problem that we couldn't solve by eating chocolate bars or running non-stop on the bush tracks.

On top of running the general store of Tryphena, Mom

and Dad managed the post office, gas station, and rental car agency, along with the telephone exchange for the whole island. We had a generator, but I still wonder how we kept the shop's fridge and freezer units cold enough at night when the generator was turned off? Or did we sell food that could kill you being half-defrosted then refrozen over and over?

It was a job for four or five people, not one couple of forty-seven and fifty-five with seven kids to raise. But Mom had that covered: older siblings and their boyfriends/husbands worked in the shop during the busy summer period. Hence my brother-in-law pulling a knife on a customer. That happened while Burke was *working*. Was it a scuffle about the postal service being late? The locals turned sour from time to time. It was all a bit *Lord of the Flies*.

We lived above the shop and school was fifty yards down the beach. We escorted ourselves to and from class even though my little brother, Sam, was barely five. We ordered meat pies for our school lunch and our afternoon snack was a Peanut Slab or a Popsicle. But we burned off this terrible calorie load by running.

Us kids ran from morning until night, unsupervised, getting in and out of mischief unaided. We were four, six and eight when we arrived and grew into seven-, nine- and eleven-year-old toughies. We reveled in our 'bush spirit' but really had no choice in it because Mom worked 24/7 and had no time to parent so she compensated by feeding us convenience food, ordering every book in the monthly Scholastic catalogue, and allowing us to go buy fish and chips every Friday night to eat out of newspaper on the beach.

Late at night when the electricity was turned off, we lay in our beds playing with lit candles, pouring as much hot wax into our palms as we could handle without crying. We went unaided on the zip line (flying fox as Kiwis call it). Wild boar crashed through the same bush tracks we played on. The dead dolphin we found on the beach one day was a tragedy to be observed for barely a minute before we eagerly watched an adult douse the dead mammal in gasoline and set it on fire. The hot springs had amoeba in it, so you weren't supposed to put your head underwater or you'd catch meningitis and die. We were careful of that, but nothing else.

We knew the drill in calamity: run and tell an adult whenever there was blood. A friend fell off the Big Swing and broke her arm, we ran to tell Mom. A boy fell off the school trampoline and cracked open his skull, we ran to tell Mom. Everything added up to a funny story and we feared nothing.

Not even the creepy old guy who made swings and zip lines so he could catch a glimpse of little girls' underpants as we flew through the air. (My sister and I figured this out and only ever wore pants.)

Of course, between the knife-wielding brother-in-law and the creepy old guy we *were* in some degree of danger. For instance, I remember Burke got into the bath with us three little kids one day. Naked.

My big sister must remember that, too, because she hollered at the locked bathroom door that he ought to come out, *now*. I remember that because I'd never seen anyone's willy, apart from my little brother's before. But that incident borders on foggy, *Xamnesian* make-believe because my brother and sister don't have any memory of this bathtub event. It took on a farcical murkiness like that scene in *Airplane* when the Captain Clarence Over has the kid in the cockpit and he says: *"You ever seen a grown man naked?"* yet the adults around them don't notice the inappropriate turn in conversation.

The bathtub thing is still something I'm not sure of. Did it happen or not? My little brother and slightly-bigger sister don't remember it. And I can't get a straight answer out of my big sister, Jocelyn—whom Burke had wooed and married—who rapped at the door hollering because she has schizophrenia and when we talk it's about entirely different topics.

What *did* happen that jolted me out of innocence and I grew a boatload of shame around (hiding from my own memory banks for a long time) was what I did on the Flagpole.

I was about eight years old and school was out, but we used to go play in the school grounds regardless and one afternoon I was there alone and climbed the school flagpole... Except the way I hitched myself up that thing, I kind of accidentally gave myself an orgasm.

And then another. And then I hung out on the flagpole for at least another ten minutes, hitching a little higher and higher, swaying in wonder at what the heck was going on down *there*.

As I mentioned, my parents worked 24/7 so I know they were blissfully unaware that their youngest daughter was getting off on a flagpole, but that metal structure was like the Eiffel Tower of the bay and I was in plain view of several houses. Mrs. Miller, the Scrimgeours (our teachers!), the Dalys, the Forresters, Mrs. White… any of them could have seen my pole-frotting. It wasn't as if the island was full of office workers, so it's a safe bet people were at home in the middle of the afternoon. And the schoolyard was on the main road. At least one car saw me, a skinny, spectacled, dirty-blonde-haired kid swaying atop the pole that sported our national flag of Union Jack plus stars.

The idea of people having *seen me* do that etched a dark groove of shame into me and was the first moment where feeling amazing linked to wanting invisibility, where enjoying life instinctively made me hide and forget.

When I told my husband about the Flagpole Incident, he doubled over with laughter, not with oh-my-god-why-did-I-marry-you disapproval, but in sympathy because he could see how innocent that whole thing was—I was eight!—and how nightmarish it is to think back on. He's been to the island, he's seen that ludicrous flagpole. He gave my hand a little squeeze when we walked past.

There were other moments of confusion about being seen or grabbing the limelight. Getting attention meant bad things.

At a community dance, for some reason still unknown to me, a huge handsome Maori guy who was lusted after by every eligible young woman there (that is, every young woman who wasn't up north shagging the cult-of-personality guy and writing postcards about it), picked *me* out of the wall of females to dance with all night long, instead of girls nearer in age.

I was flung around the dance floor like this was *Dirty Dancing*, except it was all kind of wrong because, again, I was a child of nine years old and the handsome guy was over twenty and smoking *hot*.

No adult noticed how inappropriate this was because my trusty brother-in-law Burke spiked the fruit punch with vodka so everyone there was tipsy or downright drunk and Dad almost crashed the Holden on the drive home. Mom couldn't understand why her head hurt so much the next day.

I failed to talk to anyone about how embarrassing and weird my dance performance felt. From then on I failed to tell anyone in my family anything that was too icky. To this day, my sister has to pry uncomfortable details out of me. I preferred to be a closed book, open only with friends I trusted.

But here's why Burke pulled the knife on the

customer. He sat there, legs lotus style, reading incomprehensible *Ulysses* by James Joyce, calling people out on their shameful secrets:

'Buck, we put your Jimmy Bean in a paper bag so your wife won't see!'

'Here's the dirty magazine you ordered from the mainland, Bob!'

'Your unemployment benefit's in your post office account you fraudster, Larry!'

'When are you paying your account, Steven, you owe us over $500 now!'

Until one guy threatened to slit Burke's throat if he didn't shut up. Out came the knife in reply.

Burke was into telling the truth, but he was also sneaky (i.e. that bathtub 'memory' and spiking the fruit punch). And meanwhile, by ceasing to speak up to my family about weird stuff, I didn't realize the impact on things like a sense of self-worth. I didn't see myself as important enough to mention.

2

MEN 1

A bunch of things happened: moves to and from Canada, puberty, crushing scenes of being an embarrassed geeky teen, high school scenes of horrors I'll skirt around. Many have lived that out. The years from eleven to seventeen sucked. The suicide rate in New Zealand is not good and was particularly terrible when I was fifteen. Life is so precarious. I'm lucky to have survived.

It probably didn't help that Mom maintained a 'need-to-know' basis of communication with us kids.

I never really attained the right security clearance to hear much from Mom. I'm still waiting for the birds-and-the-bees chat and when I got my period she waved me away, mumbling, "See your sister about that, she's got some *things*." Poor Mom was unable to even say: 'sanitary napkins,' let alone share instructions on tampon use.

We didn't hear a peep from Mom about boys, how to fall in love, how to send people thank-you notes or be ambitious. But we heard stories such as the time she witnessed a boy get pulverized by a Big Mac truck on the Trans-Canada highway and then rode home on her bike shaking like a leaf. Or the time she was on the St. Lawrence River in a small boat and lost the oars and was pulled downriver and almost drowned. Adventure held dangers and when bad things happened we glorified it through silence rather than talking it over as a family to sift through the hurt and heal. Mom often said, 'Remember Culloden' because she was half Scottish and that massacre by the English was meant as a present-day warning to expect annihilation and pre-commiserate it as inevitable. Family jokes and folklore were all about death.

At seventeen though, my life bloomed. Things became amazing.

I finished high school early at seventeen on account of skipping first grade because I'd taught myself to read. In February 1990, I was seventeen and a half and enrolled in an arts degree at the University of Auckland. (Downunder our school year runs February until November. Christmas is on the beach.) With the long nightmare of high school finally over, I got a blunt bob that made my eyes the size of blue saucers, took to wearing black opaque tights with mini-skirts, gorgeous secondhand cashmere tops, and started drinking *coffee*.

Before then, Mom vetoed coffee in case it stunted my growth.

I had a student allowance because my parents were

retired and lived below the means level, giving me a cool $135 per week to spend. I was still at home for most of that first year so I had the budget for film festivals and occasional group dinners out, groovy secondhand clothes, and drinking in pubs on Student Night. Thank you, Labour government! Tuition was $135 for the entire year and my high school results gave me an 'A' bursary: $200 for my course books. My only splurge was on Minnie Cooper black chunky heels. I spent money carefully but had plenty.

Auckland University was a smorgasbord of hotties. Italian classes put me in radius of the sexiest eighteen-year-old guys in the country. Guys like Adam, Paolo, several Matts and a Tristan. And the coolest girls did Italian. That's where I met 'Beautiful Fran,' Krishna, Jessica, and Miriam. These beings were incandescent and they actually spoke to me and thought I was okay.

It was a revelation.

I met other super-hip creatures through my two best friends who studied Spanish. Spanish was another hotbed of perfect ones. And don't get me started on the guys doing Shakespeare or Classical Studies or Economics. Oh my God. Every day you sat in these huge steamy lecture halls, half listening to the professor blow your mind with literary theory and postmodern analysis, half ogling the guy in the row ahead of you, willing him to turn and smile, then squirming when he did.

The guys were safe. They were funny and you could sit down anywhere in the Quad, nurse a latte from the espresso cart, strike up a conversation about nothing and they liked it and you liked it. There were no taunts from the class bully or cruel jokes made at your expense. You could sit anywhere without being vaporized with evil glares. People at university were adults. It was bliss.

My sister, Jacqui, and I started getting along better.

Throughout high school, Jac and I had issues. Maybe this was because I was two years younger but only one year behind her academically. Maybe it was her natural tendency to be the tough leader and me choosing to be her invisible maid-of-honor. But we had a thing: she was the social butterfly, I was the introvert cleverclogs. If I piped up, she put me down. And in turn, I said cutting mean things to embarrass her. Most bus trips home from school were spent hurling abuse at each other like an unscripted reality show.

But university evened things out. Jac wasn't at the same campus, she studied physiotherapy at the technical college across the harbor bridge, so she would sit in on my *Hamlet* lectures or hang out in the Quad. We'd go for lunch or coffee between classes to the Black Crow Café or Vulcan Lane. She talked to the hotties just as I did. There were never any screaming matches. We met more and more people who figured out we were sisters and loved us both. It was all very grown-up and sane.

We went out. To pubs and bars. To clubs on K'Rd. Our bestie was DTM—Don't Tell Mama—and we didn't.

Mom turned a blind eye and Dad let us borrow his car: a grunty Triumph 2500 in chocolate brown with automatic gear shift and an excellent stereo. I loved that car. I even loved it when the reverse gear broke down and we had to park so that reverse wasn't required to drive home. I always drove because Jac wasn't so crash hot behind the wheel and I could drink my vodka, lime and sodas with seemingly zero effects. The drinking age in New Zealand was twenty, not seventeen, but I had a fake ID fashioned from Jac's learner's driving permit. Oh, the confidence of youth!

At DTMs I climbed the podium nightly, in cute minidresses from This is Not a Love Shop in Mount Eden—my favorite clothes shop for its secondhand treasures. I shimmied to the early nineties techno and house. 'Groove is in the Heart' was the hit of that year, along with 'I've Got the Power' and anything by RunDMC.

I slipped into the dark spaces of Cause Célèbre and The Box on High Street, where Jac's boyfriend and friends hung out: smoking and tripping and shimmying under strobe lighting. Jac and I didn't smoke or trip but we definitely shimmied. She had a few boyfriends that year from the university set and all were gorgeous guys who smoked Dunhill Blue cigarettes, enjoyed their recreational pot, and wore hair gel. Some even modeled.

I would hesitantly stand at the bar and order my vodka, lime and soda off Kevin the Hat and hope I wouldn't be busted for being under age. But I had one of those faces that looked older being long and skinny. A horse face, I thought. With sticky-out ears. Standing beside Jac, who was beach pretty, I wasn't beach pretty. I was indie-girl interesting, I guess. I wore dramatic lipstick and curled my eyelashes but I never felt pretty. I compared myself to Jac and always, always came up short.

However, I felt useful (the chauffeur who never got drunk!), loved by my friends, and oh-so happy studying with all of those hotties.

Then I got a boyfriend.

3
___

MOVEMENT 1

The image of the airplane on the cover was important to me, but not because I've ever thrown cash out of a plane like some raging drug-lord dictator tossing subordinates from one thousand feet up. Sure, I ended up on private planes, but more importantly, airplanes and travel are the *raison d'être* of my whole family. We are Pavlov dogs: get us a ticket and we'll rock up to the boarding gate going *anywhere*, no matter the fallout.

My first international flight was when we left New Zealand for Canada in 1982. I was nine. Sam, my little brother was seven, Jacqui was eleven. The others were old enough to have left the family nest, more or less. We were leaving the island and I don't remember feeling sad about it. Mom and Dad's desperation to leave the Barrier's lawlessness overshadowed any emotions I might have entertained. We had to get away from the crap. Mom flew alone with us because Dad was held up selling the general store (they had a sale and the new owners' barge-load of furniture arrived, but their financing fell through and Dad stayed to sell for a lower amount).

Mom was a champion packer. She merrily shed everything we didn't need and streamlined our existence down to one suitcase each and two extra for household items: pots and pans, eight blue glasses bought in Mexico, crystal stemware, a brown pottery casserole dish. We emigrated without ever sending things by freight, apart from our beloved set of *Encyclopedia Britannica*. Mom slipped as many paperbacks as possible between our underpants and T-shirts and I don't recall toys following us: only a favorite teddy, doll or handcrafted Womble. We stood at check-in teetering on the edge of excess baggage. But Mom always weighed our cases and had us packed within 100 grams of the limit.

So that was us, dressed in tropical splendor, at Auckland International, boarding the first of four flights to reach Ottawa, Canada. It was mid-May. Fall in New Zealand, spring where we were headed. We were tanned little bush bunnies unaccustomed to wearing solid footwear.

The first flight, to Fiji, went fine. We had the best stopover any kid's had ever: in a motel with an outdoor pool and frogs and a gray kitten. But on the second flight, to Honolulu, Jacqui got sick.

At first it was just throwing up, which never bothered us—one of us would always be sicking up on long car trips with the hairpin bends and twisty New Zealand roads, but Jacqui's vomiting worsened on the next leg (Honolulu to Vancouver) to the point of being unable to stand up. A major meltdown was going on inside her ears. When we disgorged at Vancouver, Mom made Sam and I drag Jac around on a coat like a bile-oozing sack of contagion.

A pair of twin boys stopped beside our sorry, vomit-smeared carousel. One whispered to his brother, "Is she dead?" The other nodded, wide-eyed, "I think so."

Meanwhile Mom sobbed at Canadian Pacific's ticket counter saying we just *had* to get to Ottawa and could the lady do anything?

That's when I realized what a gifted actress our mother is. She had the airline personnel jumping through hoops. I don't know why Mom didn't want to stop in Vancouver and get medical attention, we must have had unchangeable once-or-never tickets that we'd have lost and maybe we'd missed our connecting flight, but somehow Mom's tears got us into first class on another different flight that hopped from Vancouver to Edmonton to Toronto to Ottawa. *Phew,* said Mom. I can only imagine what hell that was for Jacqui with the constant ascents and descents.

Never mind. We were onboard, hauling Jac right up to the airplane door, like a not-so-fresh trophy kill. Jacqui whimpered beside Mom for the duration. It was one of the times I saw Mom's head-stroking trick: she patted Jac's head for four hours' straight and it seemed to keep her together. Maybe in Vancouver someone had slipped someone some drugs. But meanwhile, young Sam and I enjoyed a different drug: the unsupervised luxury of first class.

First class on that flight was simply the front row of the DC 10, but we were (invisible to adults) pigging out on a tray of brandy-filled maraschino cherries.

Sam and I weaved off the plane in Ottawa half-pissed. Nobody noticed our unsteady gait beside poor Jacqui's retching and panting.

Mom actually needed a hospital after that trip. She became super dizzy at our Aunt Helen's house and spent a night in Ottawa Hospital for some unexplained malady. I blamed us kids because nobody ever explained it to us.

Result: a love for international travel that lay dormant in our blood resurfaced as a full-blown outbreak.

Mom and Dad have what I'd call a terminal case of *aviation flu*. Throughout their sixty years of marriage and childrearing, one or other would *have to go* to Canada to see a parent every year it seemed. They'd reappear three months later. The home-alone parent went into survival mode (Dad because he couldn't cook and Mom because she couldn't drive). One or other missed birthdays, illnesses, school plays, piano recitals, tooth extractions, high school exams, graduations, all sorts. It was impossible for them not to miss things because they had too many kids and their families were all back in Canada. Really far from New Zealand.

However, when we moved to Canada, they chose the eastern provinces, not Ottawa or Toronto where their family lived. Mom claims it's because she read *Anne of Green Gables* and fell in love with Prince Edward Island, just as she claims they moved to New Zealand because she read a book about the wonderful Maori people. But this strikes me as a little convenient. I think it's more that they were afflicted by a travel bug.

It goes back to the generation before them, of course, Gramma Taylor (my mother's mother) was a fierce Belfast protestant who emigrated to Canada aged twenty-one and later in life enjoyed an annual trip to Belfast until she was ninety-five. Mom's only sister married a diplomat and lived in far-flung places, so Gramma would materialize to live with them for months at a time (Japan, Zambia, Ecuador, Portugal, etc).

Dad's dad and granddad were merchant naval engineers whose logbooks detailed months away on transatlantic voyages to the Panama Canal, etc. Neither saw their family much. Dad's only brother crossed most of the world on a Vespa scooter with his wife (from England to Southeast Asia via Afghanistan in the sixties). Mom and Dad's early migrations between Canada and New Zealand in the sixties (oh, yes, they went back and forth a few times, always with a few suitcases) was achieved by ocean liner via Mexico or Western Samoa, trips that lasted six weeks and are captured on super-8 film. Oh, the fun being had by the children on the upper deck as they crossed the Equator. (The blue water glasses were bought in Mexico in 1962. The last one broke circa 1999.)

By 1994, my parents gave up on New Zealand and it became London vs. Canada in their quest to move one million times.

I'm exaggerating. It's not one million. At last count they have moved *only* sixty-six times in their married life. They just flew from London back to Canada with ninety-two-year-old Dad barely mobile and needing a commode. But they're still flying.

At a certain point, kids got left behind in countries and we have all gone for years without seeing one or other parent. I didn't see Dad for four and a half years between 1993 and 1997. It was—and is—strange. They exist as telephone voices as if we are telephone psychics in touch with departed celebrities.

Travel and movement is everything in my family.

Hence the airplane on this book's cover. That's our home. A sterile cabin in the quiet, cold part of the sky 38,000 feet up. Where it's too high to focus on the finer details.

4

MONEY 1

Pretty soon in this narrative I'll reach pivotal July 1996, when I was single once again and educated up the wazoo with a master's degree in English Literature. I received a sudden job offer and flew Pavlov-dog style, three days later, to a country I'm calling Xamnesia for the purposes of this memoir. But before I describe how I got that job offer I'd like to share about the American greenbacks floating over this book's cover. Me and money. What a disastrous union that has been.

Shortly after I arrived in Xamnesia, and a few hours before I signed a confidentiality agreement and contract to work for some people I'm legally forbidden to ever talk about, I was given a load of cash.

It is 7:03 in the morning, when a man knocks on the door and hands me and two buddies an envelope each. Thick, creamy envelopes, with a gold embossed logo that looks like an oil barrel.

We sink onto the couches, peeking. US$50,000 dollars lies inside each envelope.

Fifty *thousand*.

It's a thank-you-for-coming-to-Xamnesia tip. In the form of ten red bills of 10,000-*drachma* (let's call Xamnesia's local currency *drachma*—100,000 *drachma* equated to US$50,000). So new their numbers are still in serial order. Freshly minted money smells magical—of octopus ink and balsamic vinegar. We breathe them in, cover our torsos with them. Paper ourselves.

Before even starting work!

Like octopi, the many-armed Envelope immediately takes hold of our brains. We no longer discuss leaving (which we had been because we'd been sitting around for two weeks with no start date, plus the head of security told us we were hired to be prostitutes but weren't quite pretty enough, which freaked us out substantially). But now that we are handed a wad of cash, the comments and unclear, hazy job description don't seem to matter a bean.

I read the cash as a clear message to keep my head down and not blow this very golden opportunity. All the mystery we have encountered makes perfect sense. I see my life as pre- and post-Envelope.

I think by getting that cash I'll never be broke again. I'll remain *loaded*.

I will be broke five years from now, and I only *now* in 2015 understand what prosperity actually *is*. Clue: it's not pretty fat red bills in serial number order to paper yourself with.

But on that Envelope Morning, I am buzzing, I sing ABBA's 'Money, Money, Money' under the showerhead with squirmy, high-five-the-tiles happiness, running the water on freezing to pull myself together. I have money! A lot of money. I now have a positive net worth and a bright future. I can pay off my $8,500 college loan accrued from my master's degree—isn't that peanuts for a master's degree? To me it seemed an insurmountable amount. (And I'm talking about $8,500 New Zealand dollars. US$4,500.)

I plan on sending a chunk to my parents immediately. One of my brothers is broke. I can help *everybody*. At the time, half of my family struggles with debt and the general feeling is one of *not-enough*. (It still is. That Envelope didn't fix anybody.)

Pure motivation runs over my entire body. I decide I'm going to be the best employee that these Xamnesians have ever seen. Whatever assignment they give me I will not compare or complain. I will pick out the right combination of calm, energy, composure, intelligence, discretion, and observation to wear at all times and it will never slip off.

But guess what? I compared. I complained. My composure slipped off, often. I worked very hard, yet wondered if others were getting more money than I was, and even when I started making lots of money it didn't stay with me. I frittered it away because it made me feel bad by then. Oh, Xamnesia, you tricky, tricky fictitious place.

Banking that money means that I'm no longer Lizzie,

I'm this weird blonde creature acting a role to *deserve* those *drachmas* and more.

Yet this is not at all how I behaved around money before getting that Envelope.

In May 1993, when I was twenty, I graduated with my bachelor's degree alongside a load of the hotties. I had achieved stellar grades, even receiving a prize. I left my parent's rented bungalow aged eighteen and shared different houses with a slew of roommates, always working about twenty hours a week on top of my studies so I was never late paying rent and took care of myself, no problem.

I saved up to go backpacking through Europe. Mom gave me a one-way ticket to London for my graduation present because that's what she'd done for the rest of the kids. I got a deal through a friend who was a flight attendant with Air New Zealand so my one-way ticket was a mere 700 New Zealand dollars (US$350). I bought a 10-day Eurail pass (another US$350). And I accrued 3,000 NZD (US$1,500) through waiting tables on a floating fish restaurant and selling things I no longer needed at the Takapuna Flea Markets one cold Sunday morning.

(Although when I say 'taking care of myself' I barely ate that whole summer of being twenty because the house I shared with three messy, drunk boys and one Kiwi actress had the foulest kitchen you ever saw. Cockroaches scuttled.

The fridge pulsated with mold. We only used the kettle to boil water and pour on the cockroaches. Most days I only ate the staff meal of fish and chips before my shift, plus lemon slices dragged through a bowl of white sugar. But I looked great in my skintight black Fiorelli jeans and had very toned arms from carrying plates all day.)

My relationship *to money* was sane, at least. I didn't splurge or live beyond my means. I saved a huge amount, given how little I was paid (US$4.25 per hour, pre tax). I was proud of how well I saved. I had a goal: Europe. I didn't waste my tips in bars.

Part of this was the boyfriend. The one I found at seventeen. We were still somehow 'together' three years later. We'd only broken up once at that stage but it was a fairly toxic relationship. He'd gone to Europe alone in 1992 and I was fixated on saving *just as much* as he had. He'd left me dangling for months while he backpacked Europe, so I decided to do the same. (Except, I left on a one-way ticket, he at least had a return ticket and entrusted his car to me while he was away… but he started this whole thing. I asked him to wait one year so we could go together, but he flat-out refused.)

Backpack ready. Traveler's checks and vaccinations sorted. I was enjoying my last few days.

Then, a terrible thing happened.

Jacqui, twenty-two then, living in Brighton, UK and working as a physiotherapist, was struck by a car and lay in critical condition on life support.

It was the middle of the day. Jac waited at the side of

Old Shoreham Road, biding her time while cars passed… except a little old lady slowed to let her cross.

So she starting crossing. But never reached the other side.

The car behind, with an impatient eighteen-year-old at the wheel, overtook the slow old lady, and accelerated *smack!! bam!!* into my sister, dragging her down Old Shoreham Road for fifty yards pulverizing skull, torso, arm, then crushing her legs.

An ambulance arrived within minutes and resuscitated her twice on the way to the Royal Sussex County Hospital where she had multiple operations and was put into a coma because her brain had swollen to critical.

By the time I arrived from New Zealand (crying the whole way, a three-act odyssey taking thirty-three hours) Jacqui was the size of Buddha, green from the bruising, her hair matted with thick clots of blood, internal bleeding staunched, but legs almost amputated they were so pulped. Dad stood transfixed by the beeping monitors while Mom dabbed Arnica cream. The doctor told us she may emerge or not emerge from the coma. With brain damage, or okay, nobody could say.

The driver received a charge of reckless driving (worse than dangerous driving) when the police took in the skid marks, the scuff marks on Jacqui's shoes, and the eye-witness accounts of how the driver *failed to brake* for fifty yards.

But Jac emerged on May twenty-second from her coma.

Pretty okay.

Apart from the yelling because the head injuries made her really, really, really irate.

I sat at her bedside every day, my Eurail pass cooling its heels, my backpack unpacked in Jac's flat. I tried not to spend my hard-earned savings in expensive England where one pound equaled four New Zealand dollars. The bus fares were 27p per trip, the cups of tea in polystyrene were 12p. I sent Aerogramme letters to friends back home. I had a game with myself to spend less than £2 per day. Mom and Dad went back to Canada (their home at the time). I'm not sure why, but Dad left after three weeks, Mom after six, Jacqui was still in hospital for eleven weeks until the powers-that-be let her out 'early' because I was there as caregiver. I think Jacqui and I were worried Mom would have a stroke if she stayed any longer. Being Jac's caregiver was a crazy-making job, what with her swearing and being barely mobile on crutches. It's not that Jac swore at random things. She swore specifically at me. Me and the doctors. She kept a civil tongue around her friends. More or less.

I took on a job in the Grand Hotel in room service on the night shift because I was chewing through my savings, but it was so exhausting working from 10:00 p.m. until 4:00 a.m., then hanging out in the hospital all day that I quit after a few weeks and went on the dole for a month. (The only time I've ever signed on for unemployment.)

I'd go into her hospital room never knowing what I'd be facing: Jekyll or Hyde. But it was usually Hyde. One minute it was morphine dreams of floating on a Japanese tanker, the next it was yelling to get out. She yanked out her own feeding tube and tried to walk to the toilet down the hall on broken legs with no crutches. She convinced visitors to sneak her out of the hospital to a pub for a half pint of cider. We were back to our high school dramatics and sarcasm in front of virtual strangers.

By the end of August I had to get backpacking or lose my Eurail pass.

Jac had managed to pick up a boyfriend while in a coma (only Jac could manage such a feat! they'd been on one date before she was run over). The guy moved in with her. Phil was his name. He used to go out on drinking binges and make her hobble downstairs on crutches to make him toast and tea, with her cussing like a sailor the whole way trying to carry a breakfast tray—it was an odd relationship. So, yeah, I cleared out.

I went around Europe in a state of shock and guilt for ditching my sister even though I had just devoted three and half months to her. But I was good with my money—it lasted until the end of October. I officially ran out of funds on the Greek-Turkish border when I used the wrong passport (British) and had to pay £10 to enter Turkey. If I'd have used either my Canadian or New Zealand passport I would have paid £5.

We kids have three passports each: New Zealand, Canadian, and British. Having 'extra' passports makes us even more travel-mad. On my European backpacking adventures, I even contemplated leaving my Canadian passport with a Greek lady we'd rented a hotel room off when we couldn't find her all day to check out. We are *casual* about our passports.

My US$1,500 lasted 165 days, give or take the extra in from the hotel job and unemployment benefit, and the extra out from living in Brighton, I still managed on £4.50 or US$9 per day. This is amazing to reflect on.

That Envelope of $50,000 might have lasted the old Lizzie fifteen years. So why didn't I keep hold of it all and do something intelligent with it—like buy real estate?

Did I think the money was play money?

Did I feel that keeping my money made me a bad person?

Had I become someone who had to throw money around to feel loved and cool?

Yes to all of the above. But I didn't become that immediately. It took a while of Xamnesian conditioning. But it was already there, latently, the worry-about-others-put-off-what-Lizzie-needs reflex. I was always strapping the oxygen mask on those around me, not myself first.

Somewhere between being twenty and careful, and being twenty-three and freshly arrived in Xamnesia, money took on a murky quality and became bits of paper to assuage anxiety about my relationships, rather than what I deserved to keep for my own future. Money meant bad scary things and a load of trauma so it was better to burn through it and send it away.

I didn't seek advice from my parents about money. Whatever I shared with them came out with a big caveat: *but don't worry, I'm fine*. This was because they were so preoccupied with other kids' bigger problems. And I saw them as lacking financial acumen because they didn't own a house or surround themselves in fancy things. They didn't go out to restaurants and live it up. Yet, they lived well within their means and saved up amazingly. They traveled every year and had (have) no debt. (Or only credit card debt from sending money to financially inept kids.) Dad still jots down what they spend every day in a journal. Mom always has the readies for bailouts and loves shopping—she just prefers to shop at secondhand shops and basic supermarkets rather than expensive name brands.

I certainly didn't see money in a neutral way as something abundantly available and easily accumulated. More like an opponent I had to throw out of an airplane, with myself papered in it.

5

MYOPIA 1

When I was born, instead of screaming like a normal baby, I suspect I was thinking, *Dang, what are all these fuzzy blobs?* I'm very short-sighted, myopic, half-blind, Four-Eyed, whatever you want to call it, I can't see and people only realized this when I went to school. I probably couldn't see *way* before then and that's why I can't remember anything before the age of six.

Pre-six I have flashes of Christmases (aided by photos taken at the time) and I remember how cold or warm rooms were. Not what they looked like.

Everything was a blur.

Except for the bunny coat hook.

I have one beautiful memory of a coat hook with a bunny on it. Small and wooden, painted in cheerful colors, it seemed to say, *you belong here.* Sadly for me, it wasn't my coat hook. It was definitely Jacqui's coat hook at kindergarten because I never went to kindergarten. (And even Jacqui only attended briefly because the teacher put her in a corner and *duct-taped her mouth shut* to stop her talking during 'circle time.' Mom went ape over that. Probably my bright shiny memory of that bunny coat hook is because Mom left me in a stroller in the corridor while she railed at the teacher for duct-taping her little girl's face shut.)

At six someone twigged that Liz kept bumping into things and I got my first pair of glasses—purple-rimmed plastic. At eleven, I was fitted for rigid contact lenses. When the ophthalmologist inserted the lenses I went rigid and fainted on his russet red carpet.

Hard contact lenses held the world at arm's distance for fear of them falling out, which was a big deal because it was drummed into me that contact lenses were super expensive. It used to take me an hour to insert them, sitting on the dining table with a big magnifying mirror and towels all around me to catch the green plastic circles when my eyes inadvertently blinked and sent them flying.

To this day I have nightmares where I *must* insert large, ridiculous items into my eyes—we're talking the lids off plastic bottles, coins, and entire T-shirts. Yes, a T-shirt. *Into* my eyes.

But this isn't a memoir about my dreams.

It's about my dream-life of being in a fog. But I'm sure that part of my fog life is down to my lack of vision. I'm minus twelve diopters these days (so my focal distance is one-twelfth of a meter or 8.33 measly centimeters). There is a perpetual not-being-in-this-world dimension to being so short-sighted. I know that in the event of an apocalypse I *will be eaten by the cannibals* first and I can't catch a ball. I hate swimming. Bungee-jumping is never on the menu. Forget white water rafting. Or judo. The world is a scary place for those who can't see it.

Thus a love-hate relationship with my lenses.

They allow me to see but I get horrible grit and dust trapped under them so I often look like a drug addict with red raw orbs blinking 1,000 times per minute and unable to walk straight.

Here are my two worst grit attacks. Number one, nineteen, in Auckland, standing on a suburban street kissing that boyfriend after a party, when I got something in my eye so bad we had to knock on a stranger's door and ask to use their bathroom. The house was full of Chinese Triad guys gambling and one timid woman serving drinks. They did not want visitors and had a heated discussion while I cried on their doorstep before the woman furtively escorted me into a red-wallpapered toilet. Number two, on a street in Dominican Republic standing with my future husband, something that felt like powdered *glass* blew into my eye and I almost passed out before he got me to a café toilet.

My lenses turn me into a damsel in distress. I couldn't handle that.

I flew into Xamnesia on the morning flight of July 30, 1996. Below lay a vast expanse of yellow. The Bay of Xamnesia glittered like molten silver. As the airplane hit tarmac, the yellow came into focus as whorls of dust cartwheeling. Desert-beige dust.

Seeing dust gives me a big wallop of: *Can I survive here? Is this like the apocalypse: cannibal time?*

I try to remember how lucky I am to get this job but it feels like I've been run out of New Zealand and coming here is self-imposed exile.

I was offered the job in Xamnesia by an enigmatic Scotsman, in the restaurant I worked in, three days' prior.

I served Scottie on Tuesday night at classy Toto Restaurant with loud opera on the sound system and quality pasta. I worked there throughout my master's degree and was still there, full time, six months after graduation. Educated up the wazoo and pushing pasta. Quality pasta made of squid ink or glorious cheeses in confusing names, but still, this was not my imagined life's calling. I couldn't find a decent job in New Zealand. I had a part-time gig lecturing Television Studies at a technical college and a documentary research project, but no real job.

That boyfriend had broken up with me after five fraught years together (and as many break-ups) with the immortal line: *I love you but I'm not in love with you.* Do me a favor, dear reader. Never use this line. It's beyond cruel. It says: it's not me, it's *you*, you're just not sexy enough to keep my interest. I've grown weary of your vagina. Your breasts are blah. Your lips couldn't arouse a Viagra-popping porn fan.

That's how I took it anyway.

The trouble with any break-up was Mom. Her reaction was always extreme. Not extremely mad at whoever broke her kid's heart, but annoyed at her kid for letting somebody into her heart in the first place. Mom *told me off* for trying to sustain a relationship between the ages of seventeen and twenty-two. She said, "What were you thinking? If you weren't going to get married then why go out with him in the first place?"

It was never: "I'm sorry, my beloved child. You deserve better." It was: "You got what you asked for if you walked into that sordid sluttery without a ring on your finger." Mom believes in no sex before marriage. Or maybe even no sex within marriage. She never wants us to get hurt. But life is full of hurt and if you can't cope with it you become a pulpy mess on the floor.

So *voilà*. There I was, a pulpy mess on the floor. Dumped just before my final exams. I still had my thesis to write. I pulled off A grades, but the minute I handed in my thesis I went off the deep end. Drinking in places where that boyfriend would never go. Dragon Bar, Eastside, The Crow Bar. They were my places. I made a new bunch of friends. Friends who liked sitting on those barstools until very, very late. Good people, but party people.

Another icky thing contributed to my near-nervous breakdown of early 1996 before Scottie walked into Toto Restaurant and changed the course of my life.

I shared a villa in Herne Bay with two dear university girl friends. We were burgled on Christmas Eve. This event shook us like a snow globe because the intruder cut the phone cord beside my bed while I was asleep. (Asleep having my recurrent nightmare of inserting T-shirts *into my eyes*. Asleep without my lenses in, thus blindly, innocently asleep. If I'd awoken to see the guy snipping the phone cord, I would have no physical description to give.)

The burglary was an icky thing. It's not that he stole much, it was how he snapped the metal catch of the bathroom window in two, he was that strong, it was how he slipped into our bedrooms. One of my roommates, Helen, was in India, but the other, Jessica, was there that night and we spent Christmas Day in shock. We soon moved to different villa in Ponsonby.

We gave our statements to the police and contemplated getting a dog, but something else happened: Helen, who had been in India, spotted her stolen stereo and music collection for sale at the Takapuna Flea Markets and reported the vendor's license plate to the police. This linked our burglary to a whole series of crimes allegedly committed by the guy selling Helen's prized albums. It looked like the man who burgled us was the serial rapist terrorizing the inner western suburbs. He was codenamed 'Harvey' and in May 1996, police arrested him on twenty-seven counts of rape and one charge of murder.

'Harvey' assaulted at least twenty-seven women. More likely fifty.

Violently.

That's the guy who was in my bedroom, cutting the phone cord beside my bed while I slept.

So by May 1996, when I heard that I definitely didn't sleep much. I stayed out at night, in my cozy warm bars flanked by my pals.

The police let us know that 'Harvey' stalked us as targets by posing as one of the laborers retiling the driveway. Our landlady hired the crew, not knowing this was 'Harvey's' favorite way of scoping which houses were occupied by females only. The trio of Charlie's Angels at number 41 Wallace Street was his idea of heaven. He was hoping to catch one of us home alone.

Luckily, Jessica, came home after midnight Mass that night instead of staying over at a friend's. We saved each other. I'd contemplated sleeping on the couch at my friend's where I'd had dinner, but it wasn't far to walk home. If either Jessica or I had been home alone that night, chances are extremely high we'd have woken up trussed, about to be brutally raped.

'Harvey' followed me that Christmas Eve. I walked past a tall thin man on Jervois Road near the BP gas station, smoking a cigarette, and out of reflex I crossed to the other side of the road to put some distance between us. I kept an eye on him until I reached the turn to my street. I paused to be sure he wasn't still following. (He didn't need to. He knew me and my address by heart. Number 41. With the brand new driveway.) Once home, I locked all the doors and double-checked all the windows. When Jessica woke me up yelling at 8:00 a.m., the front door was ajar and the bathroom window's metal catch thrown across the room. I picked 'Harvey' out of the police's offered eight mug shots.

Of course I jumped at Scottie's offer of a job in Xamnesia.

Scottie was corpulent with flossy white hair and pink eyes. He paid from a roll of one hundred dollar bills thicker than a baby's arm and asked me a lot of questions in a jovial way, which I answered in a jovial way.

"Where're you from? Your accent's funny."

"From here, but my parents are Canadian."

"Do you like to travel?"

"Absolutely. I'm a 'citizen of the world.'"

He found my ability to take orders without pen and paper pretty special.

"Take my card, give me a ring in the morning. I want to offer you a job in Xamnesia," he said, with abundant rolling of his Rs.

Have I mentioned that I needed speech therapy as a child because I couldn't pronounce the letter 'R'? Myopic plus lisping, it gets better and better, right? Well, here was a guy proposing some lucrative job above the crescendos of *Tosca* and rolling his Rs like the tambours of some Shakespearean production. Fate! Destiny! Xamnesia!

Everyone had heard of Xamnesia for its oil wealth. But it's a hard country to pick out on the world map. Somewhere between Saudi Arabia and Indonesia. Generally colored yellow and the size of a tiny crescent moon. Backing onto another country where they do allow expats to drink. But Xamnesia itself is dry as a wishbone.

I didn't believe I was actually deserving of a job there, but I pocketed his card in my skintight Fiorelli jeans and agreed to meet him the following day for an interview.

I can't repeat what Scottie said in the job interview but I can assure you that no concrete details were shared as to the job or what Xamnesia would be like.

"You're obviously intelligent, Liz, you could do very well for yourself up there," Scottie divulged.

Despite the hazy details, it sounded like a boat I didn't want to miss. But I would have to leave two days later, on Friday.

Cue Pavlov-dog reaction. Airplane? Ticket? I'm there!!

I rang my parents who were in Edinburgh with Jacqui —all talk was about post-car-accident Jac (unable to cook rice without setting the pot on fire) until I squeezed a word in to explain I had a job offer in some remote fiefdom 12,000 miles away.

"As long as you hide one of your passports and keep your return ticket on you," Mom enthused. "So you can leave anytime you want."

"It sounds like a grand opportunity to build your character," Dad adds to Mom's advice, hanging up with the usual, "Thanks for that, kiddo," when I tell him I love them.

I accept Scottie's offer, arrange for a friend to take my room in the villa, leave money for electricity and whatnot, pack up and give away everything except clothes and a few books. Just like Mom when we moved, I reduce myself to two suitcases in the space of a day. I am leaving New Zealand for good.

I check in with the police detective in charge of the case against 'Harvey,' to see if I'll have to return to Auckland to testify.

"No, Miss Harwood," he says. "We'll proceed with your written statement. That ought to do it."

The detective makes a note on the file that I am leaving for Xamnesia. It's with huge relief that I board the flight to leave my home country. I have escaped the ex-boyfriend I keep bumping into. I have escaped the serial rapist who targeted me and my girlfriends.

I haven't lived in New Zealand since that July 1996 day.

'Harvey' received twenty-two years with no parole.

6

MYOPIA 2

"Stop, Miss. You open. All bag."

The customs agent regards me like it's open season on Western woman. I haven't packed so much as an aspirin after Scottie's casual mention of Xamnesia's death penalty for trafficking drugs, but watching the agent paw through my underwear has me in a blind panic.

Is he going to throw me in prison for bringing underwear into the country? Lock me up as a bra-bootlegging, tank-top trafficker?

I'm so *invested* in being in Xamnesia rather than New Zealand that I don't dare pipe up to question why he's ferreting through my things.

He puzzles over the books I've packed—checking for the wrong ideological content or bad words? I'm guilty again. They're full of both. *Fear and Loathing in Las Vegas*, Dante's *Inferno*, Graham Greene's *The Comedians*, my favorite Woolfs and Capotes. *Lolita, Generation X*. I even slipped a few favorite feminist literary essays between layers of clothing—such as Luce Irigaray, who has a nifty theory that women are in touch with themselves all the time because our labia touch. Yeah, I'm not sure why I took that sort of information to Xamnesia either. I was into French literary theory at university. Cisoux, Kristeva, Irigaray. Those chicks seemed to make some sense. The hotties in Film Studies also appreciated their gender theories. Luce Irigaray was an interesting counterpoint to Jacques Lacan's Freud-drenched hypothesis that the male phallus underpins all of Western culture.

But meanwhile, a hairy punk is still pawing through my belongings. I descend from feeling scared to feeling shame. The longer he paws, the worse I feel about the quality of my underwear. He lifts hair rollers to sniff with suspicion. He scowls at the number of lipsticks I own—as if their shiny cases are a secret warning: Western slut alert! Maybelline!! Clinique!!!

I look around. Yep, nobody else's suitcases are gutted. Western businessmen and silk-garbed Xamnesians roll past with a sneer. This is something I've attracted to myself, just as I've attracted a disastrous love life and the attentions of a violent sex offender.

Finally, I am released with no apology or smile. I can't make my carefully packed belongings fit back inside the clamped lips of my Samsonites. I wheel away with scraps of underwear for all to see.

XAMNESIA

Automatic doors open and I am in Xamnesia's real heat. That *was* air-conditioned and this *is* 100°F.

Sharp tobacco fills the air. Dried shrimp and cheap car air freshener burn nasal passages. This is a sauna perfumed with molding fruit. It's hard to breathe.

Dust hits my eyes. I freeze, blink, blind, tears roll, praying the foreign matter out. I know my eyes are now red. I look like a kid who can't behave right. Damsel-in-Distress Girl has arrived and is already blubbering.

A strange female hooks me by the elbow to propel me forward.

"Liz? I'm Hannah. What took you so long?"

Pain recedes. I blink and sniff and reassemble myself.

"Call me Lizzie."

I pluck out of the soupy air the nickname I had as a kid, shedding my school/university moniker 'Liz' in a heartbeat. That's partly because the boyfriend-of-five-years knew me as Liz. I decide right there in the foul soupy air that I'm going to be someone new as of right now.

Hannah escorts me across a broiling parking lot, filled with awfully bright Mercedes and BMWs. Is this a German section of hell? She stops at a silver BMW where a small dog pants at the barely opened window. Hannah is languid with a Marilyn-Monroe smile and a breakout of zits across her chin. But the prettiest hazel eyes.

Scottie talked about other recruits to Xamnesia. Like astronauts filling a space shuttle to be jettisoned moon-ward. Names floated like constellations, or finalists for a beauty crown. Daisy, Hannah, Charlotte, Isadora, Justine.

I feel like a finalist being one of the names. Liz. No wait, *Lizzie*. He produced a fax from 'Daisy,' that held no concrete information either. Probably to prove that no expat in Xamnesia was locked up. (Or, locked up without a fax to write sweet letters home, at least.)

"Hop in," Hannah smiles.

Cars drive with random impunity to traffic rules. Festive bunting chokes all shrubs, mummifies streetlamps and storefronts.

"Cute dog," I say.

"She's my baby, Xani. That's Xamnesian for 'Princess.'"

"Oh, do you speak Xamnesian?"

Every visible shop sells fabric, gold jewelry, or electrical gadgets. In the blur of bunting, bland buildings buckle under titanic satellite dishes. Every car on the dual carriageway is a Mercedes, BMW or 4x4 Pajero.

I realize Hannah hasn't answered my question so I try another.

"How long have you been here?"

"That's the post office. You can get your mail sent there to Daisy's P.O. box."

"Okay. Cool."

"You know, you're dressed all wrong, Lizzie…" Hannah's voice is a whisper. As if I have toilet paper stuck in my knickers in addition to my skirt tucked into stockings.

"Scottie said just cover my arms and legs out of respect for the Muslim culture…"

I'm in a white shirt and dark trousers. She's in kitten heels and a soft gray silk-mix suit.

"Yeah, but your shirt's almost see-through and those pants are too dark. Too nightclubby. You should dress like wallpaper."

Damn it, I'm already screwing up. No wonder the customs agent gave me the going over. "Right. Thanks, Hannah."

"Anytime. Remember, they give you just enough rope to hang yourself."

"Okay." Now she's freaking me out.

We park beneath a plain, white apartment block. A simple elevator opens beside the car. It reeks of baked cat's piss.

"Is this the executive apartments?"

She hands me Xani, "I'm soooooo sorry, Lizzie, but I've got to race. Go up to the fourth floor."

"But..." A desiccated gecko carcass pops under my sandal.

"I'll pick up Xani later, don't give her any meat... she's vegetarian."

7

INVISIBILITY 2

Ah, Xamnesia.

It doesn't sound so bad, does it? A bit of culture shock. A weird airport customs guy. Some chick in kitten heels with a vegetarian dog. Big deal, you're saying to yourself, what sort of numbskull allows herself to be affected or changed by a job in a place like that? They had air-conditioning, surely, where was your sense of self?

You're right, dear reader, why get dragged down? Why not remain Liz? Smart, Luce-Irigaray-reading Liz who got A grades and shimmied on the podium at Don't Tell Mama's?

I wondered if that smart, dancing Liz was really me. The five years with the boyfriend left me feeling amputated. I spent those years fitting into the mold of *his* Liz only to be ejected before I was thoroughly baked. (Literally fitting into his mold, he cast my naked torso out of plaster of Paris one Sunday, which I later smashed in anger at his *I love you but I'm just not in love with you* line.)

And I bought into Mom's narrow self-judgment: if it wasn't going to work out then why go with that boy? Sex was such a taboo in my family that I secretly wished I could dial the clock back to pre-ruining myself. Yes, messed up.

In the wake of the five-year-relationship implosion I, as I mentioned, went off the deep end. I dallied with one or two Kiwi guys who only left me feeling worse about myself because here are two fun facts about Auckland: A) it's a small population, and B) any outspoken judgment of others is whitewashed as 'protecting' your friend or 'a bit of banter.' I went into a twilight zone in early 1996 of bad choices and self-admonishment on top of certain friends' admonishment for my betterment.

There was the best friend of a friend who slept with me a few times when he was really intoxicated, but didn't like me enough to ask me out when sober. However, he did manage to ask out this other sweet, doe-eyed girl and I ran into them all the time at the bars I liked to hang out in.

There was a stand-up comedian I worked with at Greenpeace as a telemarketer. I invited him over one night. Jessica, my roommate berated me about it before he even turned up, but I was determined. In the morning, he rang his mother for a catch-up chat. I showed him these chess pieces I'd made out of FIMO (blue and pink unfortunately, the pink pawns looked like nipples). He could've cared less. What kind of self-respecting girl shows a guy her FIMO art the morning after? I was so uncool. It made the Greenpeace job harder. He picked the booth with his back to me, always, and when I rang up subscribers to sweet-talk them into supporting the whales I felt like he was judging my sales pitch. He topped the fundraising chart every night.

Then there was the restauranteur I had a 'Sunday night thing' with where we never made much conversation and he liked to smoke a joint to get in the mood. He was about ten years older than me and taught me how to flip an inside-out duvet cover onto your duvet when we'd make his bed together. I had no idea if we were in a relationship or not. Cue the sound of self-esteem shredding.

All of this added up to a bout of chlamydia and certain friends' lectures as if they owed shares in my vagina and saw its value sinking.

Attention from guys seemed to go wrong, or be badly mishandled by me and it was all my fault: just like on Great Barrier Island when that hot guy danced with me, and the old creepy guy built us swings to check out our underwear.

I flee to Xamnesia as a welcome timeout from guys.

And timeout from drinking.

It's a dry country. No boozing allowed. No vodka, lime and sodas from Kevin the Hat. No shooters lined up on the bar. No taxiing home drunk at dawn.

A curvaceous blonde with whimsical eyes opens the door on the fourth floor.

"I see you got dumped with 'Xani the Princess.' She pissed in my suitcase yesterday."

Her name is Charlotte Donnelly, and when she offers me one of her Marlboro Lights, I accept even though until today I don't smoke.

Charlotte waves her cigarette about as she gives me the tour of our digs, the curl of smoke rises as if to signal she owns pairs of designer sandals and has tossed hearts aside like dubious offerings on airline meal trays. She's tanned, wears a ring on one toe, and her jade eyes are lined with charcoal gray. We are in a three-bedroom, four-bathroom, bright white apartment.

A terrace circumnavigates the diamond-shaped building. A sluggish estuary is below. A half-dead rooster crows, followed by a static-pocked call to prayer from a loudspeaker, like at school camp.

"The phone is free," Charlotte gestures, bangles jangling.

I bee line to the telephone/fax and ring Jacqui and my parents. A free phone is like heaven. For this reason alone I am utterly in love with Xamnesia. My investment in this place ups two notches.

Charlotte hands me a can of UHT milk, instant coffee and sugar called 'Mister Coffee.' It has a mustached little Nintendo Mario-type winking at you. It tastes like 700 calories, 699 of which are saturated fats. I vow to avoid these, but am hooked on the first slurp.

We smoke Charlotte's Marlboro Lights, pig out on perfectly balled fruit: yellow watermelon, orange cantaloupe, green honeydew. It is too hot to sit on the terrace, but we do anyway, munching triangles sandwiches filled with egg mayo, tuna mayo, shredded chicken, tomato and processed yellow cheese, all stabbed with bright plastic swords from a five-year-old's birthday party. Sweat runs off our brows. Pours off the backs of our legs. I have nothing to wear for this heat.

Charlotte arrived two days ago. She's from Sydney, Australia and worked in marketing at the second-biggest radio station, but she's known Scottie 'a while' and the second he offered her a job here, she packed.

She explains that she met the key VIP in a corridor.
"What was that like?"
"Weird."
"When do start work, then?"
"No clue, Lizziegirl, I'm going to work on my tan."

Hannah drops in with another colleague dragging identical Samsonites through the door: Isadora Gibson. I recognize the name; she was the Odile in *Swan Lake* at the Aotea Centre. I remember giggling with my roommate over the one fat swan in the chorus. Isadora Gibson was definitely never going to be the one fat swan in the chorus. Everything about her is sharp—her claret bob, her cheekbones, her aquiline nose, she's one of those girls with such inner poise you feel your bravado leaching away to puddle at your ungainly feet.

"Hey there," she gives us hugs, "everyone calls me Idora."

Xani pirouettes around us, piddling.

"I'm soooo sorry, but Charlotte can you clean that up?" Hannah says, "I have to take Idora and Lizzie now. To meet the key VIP."

Idora and I run. We throw on our plain black suits (bought for us by Scottie along with the Samsonites and expense money I've almost blown all of on presents for relatives in airport shops). My hand jitters doing make-up, trying not to overdo foundation or eyeliner. Or lipstick. Or perfume.

Idora joins me, artfully dragging pink shadow over pallid eyelids.

"Hey, did you find the airport a freakshow or is it just me?"

"They went through everything," I nod. "Charlotte says that's normal."

"Hhmm. And what did Scottie tell you about a job contract? I haven't seen one yet." Idora trains her unreal blue eyes on me, whilst applying lip liner. She doesn't go over the lines. I do and have to start over.

"He said nothing." I admit. "I've hidden my passport and return ticket, in case this is all bogus."

"Good idea," she disappears to hide documents.

In the lounge, Charlotte is giving Hannah a look that reads, 'Did they just let you out of a mental hospital, sister?'

"And please don't give her any more meat," Hannah says. "She threw up last night after being here. I swear I saw beef. She's Buddhist, you know."

"I thought that was shiitake mushroom. Honest, girl,"

Charlotte fibs. I can tell it's a fib from the way she studies the end of her cigarette instead of meeting Hannah's eyes.

Hannah drives us ten miles south then a few miles east. The highway's smooth enough to eat your dinner off. It's four in the afternoon and looks as if a plague just hit. There are no people here, period. Idora asks the kind of questions I did: what's Xamnesia like? What's the job entail? And gets the same nonsense non-answers back.

"This is the Sports Club," she beams.

Fountains spray rainbow-colored water into gigantic alabaster marble basins. Huge carved wooden doors open and 68°F air freezes the trickle of sweat under my black suit. I can't describe a step further because of confidentiality clauses. However, I learned two things: A) walk on the border of the hall runner, not on the middle or else a maid would have to run after you to restore the nap because only VIPs are allowed to walk on the middle of the carpet; and B) meeting a VIP is not a long drawn-out affair. We meet our boss beside his toilet as he donned shoes. A thirty-second window to impress.

By now, you'll anticipate that I view that meeting as a colossal failure on my part. I probably did okay. Of course I did okay because I signed an employment contract after all. If the sight of me reviled someone important, I would've been on the next plane home. But already that day, I was weighing up whether Idora was doing better than me. Looking for the social butterfly to lead so I could flutter in their shadow as the one who can't handle limelight. Getting male attention meant bad things.

As I stood there waiting for the VIP to breeze through the ante-room, memories of being on national TV sloshed through me. Yet another instance of making a total dick of myself when people were looking at me too closely. When I was fifteen, I was on New Zealand's high school quiz show, *It's Academic*. I was Team Captain. We were winning. In fact, we were creaming the teams—beating private schools! I answered questions so fast I wasn't even conscious of hitting the buzzer.

But, as Team Captain I had to politely pick each envelope of questions in this rote fashion: "*Envelope Number Seven, please, Sir,*" and out of *vanity*, I wore a crusty out-of-date pair of contact lenses because I *refused* to wear my geeky glasses on television. Everything was fuzzy. I couldn't read the numbers off the board of envelopes—I was keeping track of which numbers remained by counting out which yellow blurs were left in the pockets. Towards the end of the show there weren't many yellow blurs left, I asked for the last one on the bottom row. I'd counted carefully and was positive of the number.

"Envelope Number Fifteen, please, Sir."

The Quiz Master, reaching to pluck the requested envelope, froze.

"There is no Number Fifteen. They only go up to Fourteen, that last one's the envelope of 'New Zealand Questions.'"

There was an image of a kiwi above that last envelope, but I couldn't distinguish that from my perch on the rickety set, under the white-hot lights, wearing insufficient lenses because Dad said they couldn't afford a new pair of lenses for me until maybe next year.

I died.

"I mean Envelope Number Fourteen… please… Sir."

The production team promised they'd edit it out. They didn't. For the rest of high school, the class wiseguy shrieked, "Envelope-Number-Fifteen-Please-Sir!!" like a demented parrot every time I opened my mouth. Later, the class wise-guy unfortunately died snowboarding into an avalanche in France, but at the time he made my life a misery.

It didn't matter that our school reached the final of *It's Academic* for the first time in its history. It didn't matter that I won a Texas Instruments scientific calculator and Watermark pen set. What mattered was that I looked like a savant freak who knew Stalin's birthday, the length of the Amazon compared to the Yangtze, who discovered Pi, and which famous person is buried on South Georgia—yet couldn't read numerals.

To top that wonderful experience off, I got fan mail via the school from some guy in prison. 'John.' Serving a lengthy sentence in Mount Eden Prison for I-don't-want-to-know-what. He wanted me to become his pen pal to help improve his written expression… and tell me where I lived, etc. Yep. The attention little Liz warranted was *exclusively* from criminals and deviants. The school principal told me not to respond and I'm not sure my parents even heard about 'John's' letters. He sent one or two more entreaties before giving me up as his poster girl.

So when the toilet door swings inward and the VIP's eminence (and cologne) hits us, you can bet your bottom dollar I fluff it. I'm like a sock puppet on Xanax. The sparkly wit and poise that Scottie saw in me at Toto Restaurant and recruited me for are nowhere to be seen.

Because that's what I do. Hide behind a brighter, more confident light (Idora and Hannah that day). Somehow when I was a waitress at Toto I could be witty and poised. (Possibly that's because my bosses at Toto would flail us if we didn't charm our tables. They were nothing if not disciplined about providing excellence.) Here in Xamnesia I am out of my element. I am scrambling in mid-air like a cartoon cat.

The VIP catches my eye. *She's nervous.* I see it register in his mind. His face transforms to empathy—like rapid-moving clouds over a field of yellow. He brightens when he senses shame. My squirminess is an elephant in the room. 'But there, there,' his benevolent look says, 'you're not going to die.'

This makes me squirm even more. I can't handle empathy. It's like dust. Even microscopic, it makes me tear up and wish it would stop.

As soon as he leaves, Hannah leads us back to her car and deposit us back to our apartment sinkhole. "Well," she says. "I don't know where they'll stick you two, there's no property that actually needs anybody."

I don't mind hanging out in the apartment like a slowly rotting papaya. As long as I can stay here, hiding under a rock if need be. Just don't send me back home.

8

MISCHIEF 1

We watch the sunset from the terrace. It is still gluey hot.

Scottie failed to mention foreigners are allowed to enter Xamnesia with two bottles of alcohol. Charlotte is savvy enough to know the alcohol laws of every country in the world and has two liters of Smirnoff Blue stashed in the freezer.

Idora, conforming to her mother's ambitions, danced all her life until she injured her back a year ago. Now she can only teach but has big plans to open her own studio.

"Mother's going to help me run it," Idora says grimly.

"Brave. I can't imagine even running a lemonade stand with my mother," Charlotte's jade eyes widen.

Idora pours more vodka, drizzling Red Bull, melon balls plopping as garnish. She and Charlotte are entirely relaxed here, apart from our jokey concerns of this being some white sex slave ring. "Mother's already picked out the width of the oak floorboards, the color of the wall behind the welcome desk and the thickness of the towels in the changing room. She practically pushed me on the plane here…Why did you two take the job? Do you think this is the smartest thing we've ever done or the dumbest?"

"I'm here because Scottie promised it's going to be brilliant," Charlotte says. "And I wanted to get as far away from my ex as possible. He did my nut in."

"I just broke up after a two-year thing," Idora pokes at her melon garnish, misty-eyed for a moment. "Distance is good."

I add to the confessions. "Five years and he broke up with me right before my final exams. But that was six months' ago. I'm over it," I say, sham that I am.

"Cruel," Charlotte says.

"Well, I still got As. He got Bs. But that's not why I came up. I want to save enough money so I can go sit in a village somewhere and write…"

"I'd love to read something you've written," Charlotte says.

"Same," Idora says. "Teaching wasn't the top of my list, but I actually want to teach girls more than how to dance. I want to teach them how to stand up straight and look the world in the eye and be okay with themselves. Ballet can crush your spirit."

"That's cool. I don't have a beautiful career plan, as such," Charlotte palms her pink lighter repeatedly—a nervous tic I notice she does when she's feeling ill-at-ease. "I left Sydney before, but it didn't stick. This time I want to stay gone."

Writing is my secret ace up my sleeve. Or so I believe.

At university, I was accepted into the Creative Writing paper that only accepted a dozen applicants. One woman, Kristin, pulled out so I was lucky number thirteen. It felt like a benediction and I loved that class, receiving an A there, too. Even for my shocking poetry.

I'd always loved writing. I wrote an epic fantasy called *Arealmia* when I was thirteen with two friends from middle grade. It involved a secret whirlpool that transported the main characters (star-crossed lovers, Farra and Teltian) clear across the bedeviled land of Arealmia. (See, even my characters were fixated with travel.) Everyone had super powers they used for good or evil.

Later, I wrote murder mystery dinner parties during the university years to play with a mix of my and Jacqui's friends. Our first murder was such a success that Jacqui slapped me across the face! She didn't like how everyone praised me for my hidden writing talent. That led to a tearful screaming fight just like when we were on the school bus and after that I was reluctant to 'show off' things I'd written around Jac.

After university, somehow between finishing my thesis and all the late nights and off-the-deep-end behavior, I started getting short stories published and received a $2,000-dollar grant toward the completion of my first novel.

So when I went to Xamnesia, I had recently received that grant and planned to write when I wasn't toiling for the VIPs. I committed to a 100-hour per week job plus added a second career on top without a thought for how I would actually manage that, physically or emotionally. I knew I wanted to be a writer. Taking a job to earn lots of money in a tax-free country seemed the best way to be a writer: life experience plus easy savings so that I could go live in a village and write... *later*.

After Xamnesia, my real life (as an author) could begin. Part of being in a state of Xamnesia is that you'll happily delay your true goals to take the easy path. That's part of the feeling invisible yet invincible. You are cocooned into putting off the hard work to make a dream into a reality. Thus the validation I'd already received for my writing only encouraged the head-in-sand blinkering to reality.

Am I ever lucky to have met Charlotte and Idora. I already half idolize them. We turn up the volume on the music. Approve of each others' CD collections and framed photos: Charlotte's colorful foreign cityscapes; Idora's black-and-white dancing portraits and her kid brothers; my photos of siblings, dead cats, and me hugging pals.

Charlotte has 500 CDs and 100 gorgeous bangles.

Idora also has a wicked CD collection, possesses only black underwear, and brought thigh-high boots simply because she couldn't part with them.

My belongings look like arbitrary hand-me-downs in

comparison, but they kindly admire my russet dressing gown that belonged to my grandpa, Harry Harwood. The kind of dressing gown worn by men who smoke pipes.

"I used to write in that," I explain. "As a lucky charm." I turn to Idora, "What happens when you wear white… if you only have black bras?"

Her sharp eyebrows rise, "I *don't*."

Idora's entire wardrobe is navy, black, and charcoal. I tell them Hannah's advice to dress 'like wallpaper' and we lose it laughing. When I add the info Hannah shared, about how 'they' give us 'just enough rope to hang ourselves,' we're on the floor.

Charlotte and I decide to go for a walk. Idora is content to stretch for a few hours—to stay limber. But we're antsy. Big mistake.

There is no sidewalk, no bus stops, no street signs, not even a passing taxi. Only sporadic concrete islands like broken pack ice. We skirt dead rats, cicada husks, dusty Coke cans. Young Xamnesian lads hang out their Mercedes windows whooping, "I love you!!!!" and "Hello Girl!!!!" The heat weighs on us like gravity on Jupiter, like we wear concrete flip-flops. I'm shocked at how shitty and dusty normal Xamnesia is compared to what we saw at the Sports Club. Isn't this supposed to be the home of the superrich? Why isn't the whole place more spruced up?

We stumble upon a collection of shops. The biggest

signs of life are the unfixed cats with no tails. Where are the people? We find a grocer's run by an Indian gentleman in a maroon turban.

On the return hike, dewy cans of tonic and packets of cigarettes swinging in thin plastic bags, a black BMW almost knocks me into a storm drain.

"Get in!" a girl hisses. "I'm Daisy. Get in!"

"What is it?" Charlotte asks.

"You cannot walk around like that! Look!"

A cavalcade of outriders on motorbikes, black Bentley, black Porsche, two Mercedes and more outriders scream past going eighty miles an hour.

"Who was that?" Charlotte says.

"A VIP," Daisy sniffs.

Daisy wears a diamond Rolex that could snap her wrist in two. She is eating-disorder thin.

"You can't be seen walking around." She halts at the end of our driveway. "There's a shop that way around the next corner."

"We can't be seen…?"

"I don't have time for this," Daisy says. "Whitney's performing tonight for the general public. Be ready at 6.30 sharp."

By 7.30 p.m., with no sign of Daisy, we're sure this is her sick idea of a joke. Unless we've already been fired (before starting our jobs) and nobody bothered to inform us. Charlotte is willing to go for another walk to get picked up by *anybody*. And which 'Whitney' was she referring to anyway?

"Let's see if we can hitch a ride with a Mercedes full

of teenagers," Charlotte stews, picking at the hem of her shirt.

Finally, Daisy rings on the apartment phone to order us downstairs.

"You're dressed completely wrong," she states.

Our crime is blue jeans and black tops.

"You said it's a concert for the general public though?"

"Yeah. Still."

It seems that everything we do is watched and reflects on our suitability to stay here.

Daisy's in a mushroom gray pant suit. Diamonds hang from her earlobes like cowbells.

"Surely they'll be looking at the stage?" Idora says.

"Never mind."

I feel sorry for Daisy's bitterness about blue jeans. Why should she care if we look a little casual? Scottie told me she's twenty-one. That makes us three (twenty-four) a *little* more street smart, doesn't it? Nope. It does not.

I try small talk, not understanding only a platinum crowbar could pry Daisy open. She won't even admit what country she's from.

"Which VIP do you work for?" Charlotte tries.

No reply.

"What do you actually *do*?" I persist.

"Where did Scottie find you? I told him to find smart girls. You won't last a month here."

She told Scottie what type to recruit? What kind of power does this Daisy have here? Charlotte, Idora and I stare out the windows for the remainder of the journey.

Daisy parks near a twelve-foot high gate reading: 'Playground' in what I'm guessing is real gold painted onto the black wrought iron.

The paths are paved with real marble and a giant musical fountain shoots a spray of water lit with rainbow colors in a Salomés dance in synch to 'When I Fall in Love' by Nat King Cole. Weird. This is the Land of Oz, in the desert. What is their water bill like?

"Where are the mosquitoes?" Idora asks.

"Gardeners pump chemicals in the air to kill them," Daisy says.

Not so much as a cicada chirps.

"Are Hannah or Justine coming along?" I ask.

Daisy flicks her ponytail close to my eyes, "Justine's in charge of the property where Whitney's staying, so she has to stay there on Standby."

"Standby what?" I know I really ought to shut up, but I can't stop myself.

"It's called being 'on Standby,'" Daisy says. "Something you'll never do the rate you're going."

"And Hannah?" Charlotte asks. Daisy lets the question hang.

We arrive at an open amphitheatre where a few thousand people sit in rows as calm as cows in a meadow. Hardly a concert vibe. Daisy shoves tickets at us and disappears.

We find our seats, chattering now we are out of Daisy's hearing. Her attitude doesn't faze me. I'm accustomed to mean-talking girls. If she wants to be Type A so be it. I figure she'll warm up once we're all working together.

Whitney bursts onstage—it is Whitney Houston—in a gold dress so tight she needs stagehands to lift her down to the lower apron. Her voice rains over us like gold coins on a platter. Lights dazzle. Mini-fireworks explode behind her frizzy halo. It's a shame I don't like her music. But it's infectiously upbeat and her voice cuts straight through the soupy air to make our senses come to life. Soon the three of us stand up, clapping and shimmying.

"Her voice is amazing," Idora shouts.

"Her hair looks like a wig," I shout back.

Whitney doggedly encourages everyone to dance, but everyone remains seated. We whoop a little. I can't believe the audience is so pulseless.

But between 'I Want to Dance with Somebody' and 'How Will I Know?' the man in front of us gets a phone call and swivels in our direction.

"Sit down!! Sit down, now!!!"

We sit like we've been punched in the guts.

The man holds out his phone through which we clearly hear male screaming. *VIP hollering*. It lasts one long minute until whoever it is hangs up.

"Stay in your seats," the man orders.

"Was that a VIP?" I ask.

No reply.

Thinking back, it was probably a right-hand guy and not an actual VIP. Why would the special ones deign to lose their rag over the three of us shimmying innocently high up in the bandstands? The right-hand guys always lost their rag *on behalf* of the VIPs. That was their job and they were loud at it.

We slink so low that we're horizontal and the rest of Whitney's high Fs wash over us like white noise. Even when she gets some VIP young couple in the front row to stand so the public can cheer (approaching and talking to them like they might spontaneously combust, 'Oh? You're shy? It's okay...'), we clap with extreme caution. This being 1996, everything was a once-experienced event. We had no Internet with which to share things or contextualize or simply vent.

At the end, Idora whispers, "This place is weird."

"Fucked, more like," Charlotte amends.

We wait beside Daisy's car, deflated.

She approaches, "You're lucky you're not already on a plane back to your pathetic lives wherever it is you're from."

"You're right," we chorus, meek. "We had no idea."

"I have to go to Late Party. A driver will pick you up." She wastes no time driving off.

When all the locals disperse into the muggy darkness and we are still propping up the black-and-gold gate with no driver in sight, we finally burst out laughing.

"What the fuck?" Charlotte says.

"If we're being deported somebody needs to at least drop us at the airport."

We shake with hysterics, but feel like idiots. It's like I don't understand *English* anymore. I am *invested* in this being a real doable job. It feels like it's cannibal time and

I'm blind to life-saving nuances. A silent driver drops us at the apartment.

Out on the terrace, we huddle over long fingers of Smirnoff. Charlotte and I smoke. We listen to the broo-ha-has of wild dogs in the pitch-black. Xani curls between us, her ribcage rising and falling in bliss.

"We need to look out for each other," Idora pronounces.

Charlotte sighs, "I'll ring Scottie again tomorrow. If we could just start our jobs then we'll be too busy to get into mischief."

But that isn't really true.

Starting our jobs doesn't keep us out of mischief at all.

9

SILENCE 1

It's drummed into us *not to talk about anything*. Everything is bugged, we hear. Everything is a black mark against your name. Certain words spoken on the phone lines trip listening devices. Words like 'sheikh,' 'king,' 'princess.'

I quickly turn weird in my faxes and letters.

Friends start writing things like: "Are you alright? You don't sound like yourself."

The thing is I wasn't myself for about six months *before* I went to Xamnesia, so I certainly wasn't any *more* myself hanging out in the desert with a bunch of sheikhs.

Nuh-uh.

The place wasn't some Nirvana to *find yourself* in.

Maybe the trauma of Jac's accident was part of this. That event had untethered me so much. Before she was pulverized by that Peugeot 207, I was a braver person. After that, being alone meant being vulnerable. I hated to eat alone in a restaurant or café. I walked around like one of those urban-myth humans who spontaneously combust for no earthly reason.

I talked to the university psychologist for a while when I was freshly returned to New Zealand for my master's degree and found myself crying a lot and unable to concentrate during lectures. I'd also put on about ten pounds living in Europe and reuniting with that boyfriend had been a weird 'Well, you're back so I guess we're still together' unsexy reunion. The boyfriend looked at me with distrust because I'd hung out with a cute German guy called Franck for one night in Brighton. Lord knows I needed the diversion from the Jac Circus at the time. But I suppose the boyfriend's trust in me was in shreds, even though Franck and I only kissed, a lot. Nothing more. And spent the night cuddling. Yeah, I guess I deserved the frosty welcome back.

The shrink deemed I had post traumatic stress syndrome, which at the time meant nothing to anyone and I had no idea what to do with that other than stick like glue to the boyfriend in some hope that sustaining that relationship would erase the hard days with Jac in Brighton. (And erase his image of me cuddling the German.) To this day, when I see anything too medical involving a pulpy mess of blood I need to sip a Coke immediately or I throw up, as I threw up at the Royal Sussex County Hospital when they would change poor Jac's dressings on her legs after the bone grafts and skin grafts. Even the word 'graft' made me feel sick. Yet that's what I did: grafted myself on that boyfriend as if existing independently would be my death.

When Idora, Charlotte and I start work, finally(!), after the Fifty-Thousand-Dollar Envelope, the relief is palpable. I can breathe again. I'm given a cell phone and a midnight blue BMW as company car. I navigate the roads carefully because the VIPs are used to having their roads all to themselves and I'm paranoid I'll smash head-on into one of the wives, but I'm in love with my car. *In love*. It has a five-CD changer and I smoke in it, window rolled down to the sultry air.

"I have a problem," Charlotte confesses on our first day on the job, back at the apartment. "I don't know how to drive. I made up a story to get a driver to drop me here in my car."

"You've got an automatic? It's just steering. I'll teach you."

Her car is beyond beautiful. An olive green C-class Mercedes with only twenty miles on the clock. The cream leather interior and glossy walnut paneling are softer than baby's skin. I inhale the new car smell and try not to compare that I was given a secondhand BMW with three thousand miles on it already to Charlotte getting a new Mercedes. Does that mean something? Have I been given a dud property to manage? Charlotte was allocated a mini palace where foreign heads of state stay when they visit. But then again, Hannah's in a silver Toyota Crown and seems to be doing great. We've been told 'Don't compare' about twenty-million times, but that particular rule doesn't seem to stick in my head.

"I learned. I just never got around to sitting my practical," Charlotte says.

"It's really easy. You forget your left foot. And go easy on the gas. The captain of security at my house said there's no point us getting Xamnesian driving licenses. The police never pull anyone over. They're too busy being outriders for the VIPs. All we need is our ID cards that say who we work for."

"Amen to that."

Charlotte eases the car forward and we start with turns in the wide concrete parking area below Seven Story White Building. That's what our home is called. Just as there are no street signs here, the roads aren't named and there are no house numbers either. Things are unlabeled. Our building sits on a long soulless stretch between the airport and the VIPs mansions with no shops within walking distance except the tin shack 500 yards down that sells instant noodles, Garfield merchandise, zero alcohol, ballpoint pens and dried fish that stare up at us with their flat dead eyes as if to say: *'You're screwing this up already, numbskull.'* That's our 'hood.

After several figure-eights I encourage Charlotte to head out onto the highway we have to drive on to reach our places of work. She's a great driver, if a little too considerate compared to the concrete-footed locals, and the sound of her indicators spooks her into almost rear-ending a Mercedes in front of us. We heard that if we get into a prang with a local Xamnesian we'll be instantly deported.

"You're a natural!" I say as Charlotte glides into a

park outside Happiness Apartments. That's where Daisy and another girl, Justine, live, along with seven other floors of entourage: physiotherapists, speech therapists, private tutors, personal assistants. It's the address for those who are doing well here. Our building is for the newbie's (and Hannah), those on probation, until someone deems we've passed some unwritten evaluation.

"Okay, but you're driving us home." Charlotte lights up a cigarette to celebrate passing her Lizzie-certified driving test.

Daisy phones inviting us up to her apartment, where a long rack of suits awaits. A gift from the VIPs. I think, wow, I don't deserve Emporio Armani, Maxmara and DKNY! But really, we are representing *them* and it's a job so we need to look professional and these people are probably spending half a million per day. This is less than nothing to them. I tie myself in knots at each gift, each bestowment (the cell phone! I've never had one before), the car (it's a flipping BMW! Sayonara Dad's Triumph 2500). The others receive things with quiet self-confidence of *deserving this plus more*. They are used to good treatment. Idora's from a good family. Charlotte's folks live in Double Bay, the posh part of Sydney. I'm used to rummaging the baskets of This is Not a Love Shop for a treasure and accounting for all dollars and cents to cover my rent.

"How was day one on the job, girls?" Hannah's already there, flicking through the rack. "What's your pant size, Lizzie? I always need a bigger jacket and small pants—you're the opposite, right?"

That's Hannah's way of referring to my pear shape compared to her Barbie doll figure. That's another thing. I have a bigger booty than the others. It has to be said. I am not as pretty. I am the indie-girl, Betty-Davis-eyed 'interesting' one, not beautiful like the others. I've put on a few pounds in water retention or something. I feel too bulky for my skin. This is me comparing myself unfavorably to others because I started that trip early due to my weird sibling rivalry with beach-pretty Jacqui.

"Day one was fine," I tell Hannah. Day one on the job consisted of a five-hour indoctrination by the captain of security at my property warning me to *never talk about anything*. I will never talk about the Picassos, Monets, and Modiglianis in a gloomy private museum I spotted earlier that day. Or that my codename used by the guards at my property is apparently 'Cinderella.'

Calvin Klein, DKNY, Giorgio Armani, D&G, Helmut Lang, Chloë, Emporio Armani, Ralph Lauren, Bruno Magli, Emenegildo Zegna, Escada, and Max & Co. The suits were flown in from some nearby country because Xamnesia flies everything in, including the milk, and the sizes are definitely Asian. Or French. They're not New Zealand sizes at any rate. I vow to start going to the gym I heard we are allowed to go to. Or smoke way more and eat way less.

There are shoes for us, too. Elegant Ballys, Bottega Venetos, and Salvatore Ferragamos. But no purses. We've already realized that all we need are our hands to hold our cell phone. Nothing should ever be written down so there's no need to cart around to-do lists or agendas. I have a filing cabinet in my office that will remain barren. Car keys can be left in an office or even the ignition. It isn't like anyone's going to steal anything here when the locals have about two Mercedes each and with the death penalty for drug smuggling who knows what punishment is dished out for auto theft?

After our spree, Idora, Charlotte and I sneak off to a certain Chinese restaurant 'downtown' Hannah told us about and order 'special tea': beer served in a teapot (forgetting my vow to starve myself as I zipped up the Helmut Lang stovetops). Hannah seems to know where to go to have a little bit of fun.

I drive Charlotte's beautiful Mercedes back to our 'Loser's Building' and fall into bed happy. I survived my first day at work without getting deported and have scored six new business suits. Xamnesia is an amazing place. I am so *lucky*.

10

SILENCE 2

My stomach's a bottomless pit of eels. Tonight we have to work at a function, whatever that is.

At the Sports Club, Justine appears to show us the ropes. Another name that was floated by Scottie. She lives at Happiness Apartments.

"I've been go-go-go the minute I arrived," is the first thing Justine says.

She's a regular chatterbox compared to snarky Daisy and smiling no-info Hannah. Her frizzy black halo, ski jump nose, and plump cheeks suggest she's up for anything and you better believe she's your girl for the job. Within one minute she tells us that she's '*just* turned twenty-two,' studied hotel management, her dad owns racehorses, and she was the only person recruited from an advertisement they ran in *The Vancouver Sun* for a 'Waitress in Asia.' But the fact that she's Canadian, like my Mom, makes me instantly warm to her.

It has to be said that I would never have applied for a

job advertisement like that. It sounds like a code for drug mule or sex slave. This is Justine though. She tells you something and you end up nodding along instead of interrupting with a: *What the hell?* She is *very* compelling. And enthusiastic.

"Two hundred applicants—I'm the only one they took."

She wears a long pinstriped skirt with matching jacket. I thought we were supposed to stick to pants, not skirts here, not even long ones. Idora and Charlotte shrug, glancing at each other. They think she's full of shit.

"Did you guys do something to your hair?" Justine frowns. How did she know?

My hair looks more sodden mouse fur, not 'Golden Splendor' as the box promised. Idora's is like a synthetic black wig. Charlotte's has lost its sheen. We are so paranoid about fitting in with the 'wallpaper' look that today we dyed each other's hair. Idora also gave me a haircut. A chunky layered do, way beyond any style era any of us could describe. I look like a runaway from a dystopian sci-fi movie. The hair dye was found in the tin shack grocer's down the road and expired in November 1995.

Inside the Sports Club, it's the fridge-like chill again. All we learn that night is that Justine's effervescence makes her loved by all the function staff. I learn how 600 people eat their main course at exactly the same time: sixty giant Lazy Suzans in the middle of the tables keeping exotic dishes warm. I smell durian, or jackfruit, which is the most disgusting thing ever. And at the end of the night, we overhear some high-up entourage say to Hannah:

"You can drive the girls home because you don't have to go to Late Party anymore."

To which, Hannah's pretty hazel eyes fade like a bunny whose neck's been snapped.

Late Party is some sort of big deal. You'd think Hannah would be pleased to catch up on some sleep rather than drag her ass to that every night from midnight till 3:00 a.m. But, apparently not.

Her baby doll lips quiver on the trip home, "Justine's going to Late Party now. Never forget girls, nobody's irreplaceable."

Hannah sticks around for a drink, as animated as a maced mullet, and stares at our swimsuits drying over the terrace railing, "They just sacked a load of maids because they hung their washing out on the balconies and someone drove past and saw their underwear..." her voice reduces to a hushed mumble.

Daisy drops by for a Mister Coffee. I think she's been told to instill us with the 'right' ideas:

Don't think you're special; your position can change overnight.
Don't leave your cell phone, even for a second.
Don't let someone else answer your cell phone.
Don't tell people you're tired.
Don't tell anyone anything.

But after those Envelopes of Cash, the good sense

trickles right out of our heads along with our objectivity, leaving blissful indoctrination.

What's that, dear reader? *You* want to know what the job was actually like? Who these VIPs were and how many VIPs we're talking about? What they terminated staff for? Their caprices and weak spots? What kind of movies they watched from their gigantic beds? What kind of exotic pelt their bed throw was made from? What they spent in an afternoon shopping? Did they require surgery?

I could tell you, but I'd have to kill you.

Blame clause #15 of my contract for that.

I slump at my desk. My reflection jumps out at me in the six-foot tall unwanted Venetian mirror propped up against my office wall. How long can I last now I'm inside a property on my own?

I already miss Idora and Charlotte and we only met two weeks ago. Why can't I function?

When you grow up at the tail end of seven kids, you're never left to your own devices. You sleep in bunk beds until you're seventeen and opt to leave home altogether. You finish your dinner because there is no way mom is making you a special meal and your brother will eat it if you don't. So when you're left alone, you panic. Or at least, I did.

I existed in a pack, even if it was a pack that tended to claw each other when nobody was looking. I sought out a new pack wherever I went: at the multiple schools I attended, in those golden years of university where I finally came to life, at all my part-time jobs where I busted a gut, even my roommates—there were always at least three of us and I tried to be everyone's best friend even when I was falling apart at the seams. I bonded here with Idora and Charlotte within hours.

Truth is, I surround myself in company constantly. I'm always on the lookout for a new best friend, like a phantom fake twin (which I actually had when I was born, I'll tell you about it later). Until I have a new pack, I am a fish drowning in air. The people inside the property I'm 'managing' aren't my pack.

The security captain and his guards aren't my 'big brothers' unless in the George-Orwell-surveillance sense. The household staff of one hundred maids, waitresses, laundry and kitchen help are lovely Thai people. Maybe they can be my pack.

I go out the back door of the kitchen to smoke cigarettes and chat to the cooks and kitchen hands who call me Miss Lizzie. It's laughable. I am a 'Miss.'

11

INVISIBILITY 3

The VIP who lives at my property arrives home from some diplomatic wanderings. (Or shopping, I can't tell you either way.) I must stand with Captain and Mr. Malik in the Foyer to bow when the VIP walks in. Shudder. I don't like being visible. Even for a second.

I ate too many instant noodles for lunch; I can only take in spoonfuls of air. The frankincense they pump through the air vents makes my head hazy. The coffee I gulped feels like setting concrete in my stomach.

Towering beside me is Mr. Malik, one of the right-hand guys. The whole country rings him. He has three cell phones and reportedly sleeps a total of two hours per night. That's half what Leonardo da Vinci got. He looks part-Persian, part-Machiavelli, with his black hair receding into a W, mercilessly trimmed salt-and-pepper beard, and eyes on fire with authority. There's a word in Maori (New Zealand's indigenous language): *mana*. It is power and prestige, it's supernatural and possibly located near the testicles. Mr. Malik has bags of the stuff.

He eyes me in the reflection of the wall of windows opposite while he hollers into a phone, turning cardiac magenta. I feel like I'm about to make a right boob of myself. Again these powerful men give me flashbacks of every moment that has squashed my sense of self.

One school play, when we lived in Canada, when I was twelve, I got the lead role. Go, little Liz! I was the 'Empress' in an all-female version of *The Emperor's New Clothes*. (Not because I went to a single-sex school, but because no boys wanted to be onstage with us thespian losers.) At twelve I had no breasts, only ghostly white limbs, buckteeth, mousy hair, and my blinkety-blink hard contact lenses making my life a precarious hell.

I was supposed to have a flesh-colored bodysuit for the nude scene, but the inept wardrobe mistress (the teacher) could only rustle up navy blue. So in the scene when the Empress appears in her 'clothes' but really she's naked and you really need a flesh-colored leotard, I stood under the hot lights in *navy*.

The whole auditorium, teachers included, lost it laughing. I needed the script prompt: "Is this my ruby and ermine robe? It's so light… I feel as though I'm wearing nothing but my underwear…" and Corey Delaney who I had a burning crush on called from the darkness, "Hey Geek, are you part Smurf or just frigid?" After that I wasn't blue anymore—I was bright pink.

Mom, on the ride home in our Ford Pinto, said, "Didn't you *know* you were supposed to wear a flesh-colored leotard? How were we supposed to watch you in what you had on?"

Dad shook at the wheel laughing, wiping tears of laughter, "That was some show you put on."

Mr. Malik says a bit more in his native language (whatever it is, it makes small talk sound like long talk as all compound nouns take ages to articulate). From his tone, I guess he's saying something like: *Sort it out you motherfucking cocksucker or I will come over and insert your cell phone into your rectal cavity*!

Everything is silent. Mr. Malik's eyes on me are like a magnifying glass burning up ants, "This house very important house," he growls. "It is the hub. All the little spokes come off the hub. If the hub come apart and the spokes come off, the whole motherfucking wheel come off and then we all get fucked by the spokes."

He scares the bejesus out of me. I nod.

Hannah is fired. Or 'let go.' The two terms are interchangeable around here. The story (recounted by compelling Justine) is that she was seen rollerskating around the Playground on Sunday morning in a tank top and shorts.

It's not clear who saw her but it's grounds for sacking. Did she do this on purpose, I wonder? She seems to have lost all will to remain in Xamnesia ever since she hasn't had to go to Late Party.

She throws herself a farewell party and bequeaths us

Xani, which we aren't that thrilled about and quickly find her a more appropriate tribe, the Western chief of security with his twin boys who love having a puppy. But we are thrilled about drinking her stash of Dom Pérignon while she packs five Samsonites, her cheeks raw and eyes liquid. Idora, Charlotte and I are the only party attendees. Daisy's busy and Justine has President Suharto to Standby for.

"My dad gave me hell about being let go—they've just put down a deposit on a yacht," Hannah says, tears rolling.

"Don't ever think you know best!" she declares.

"And girls, don't, ever, change for this place," she adds, sitting on her Samsonites to close them.

She confesses she's been here five months and has made a quarter of a million, but doesn't want to go into 'further' details (those details were enough for us!).

"Remember about the rope," she adds, dumping a load of diamond watches into a free-with-purchase toiletry bag.

My world distills to the distance between Seven Story White Building and my property (let's call it *House X* for ease of remembrance).

Free time swirls down a vortex at Seven Story White Building where Idora, Charlotte and I hunch over the dining table, pad of paper and pens at the ready (because we believe that everywhere is bugged), scribbling what we've gleaned about the VIPs, gossiping and lighting our cigarettes off the gas rings in the humid, florescent kitchen where tiger moths lurk and geckos cling to the walls. The kitchen is the only room without air-conditioning and it's never used for cooking, only lighting cigarettes and mixing drinks.

I turn twenty-four, and receive a fax from my closest friends who threw a birthday party in my honor with everyone taking turns at the computer to write me messages. It makes me cry. We celebrate the only way we know how—cracking open a Red Bull to mix with the last dregs of vodka and going on a few amusement rides at the perpetually quiet Playground. Dizzy Again is our favorite ride, where you are strapped onto a giant phallus and dropped from a great height. If that ride ever malfunctioned it would surely smash your legs to smithereens.

My pack of Thai bakers make me a heart-shaped cake with icing so thick and creamy it's literally lard. It haunts our empty fridge for three weeks, hanging out with the nail polish, face masks and the half lemon we've christened 'Bob.' It tastes the same on day twenty as day one. We tunnel through the sponge in spoonfuls, not slices. Even birthday cake in Xamnesia is unreal: hollowed out.

I put in huge hours at House X. Mainly invisible. Sitting in the service kitchen during important mealtimes with somebody's female bodyguard sitting opposite (a high turnover role performed by an Asian former policewoman usually doing needlepoint kittens on cushions for her impending wedding). The VIPs eat in the next room and I don't even know who is in there with the key VIP. The ickiest and most expensive thing on the menu is bird's nest soup which costs US$50,000 per bowl and is made from the saliva and vomit of special birds who dwell in hidden caves in Indonesia. The nests are harvested at great risk to the poor guys on forty-foot high ladders.

It's a bubble within a bubble. The only link to the real world I have are disembodied voices of employees in other countries. After each contact I have with these faceless creatures I applaud myself, thinking I am finding my feet. The only data required is cell phone and fax numbers. None of us works by e-mail; texting isn't happening in 1996. People are rung at any hour o'clock, seven days a week. Every instruction handed down is treated with life-or-death urgency.

I'll get a phone call at 2:00 a.m.:

"Lizzie, remove the Lafartique. Thank you."

That means one of the three after-shave fluids that graces every gold-tapped bathroom across ten properties here and another twenty overseas must be culled before the VIP next uses the loo. The toiletry line-up alters slightly depending on what country a VIP is in (different sunscreen in the Philippines to Las Vegas, say), but in general about fifty products are arranged in the exact same way, globally. If I close my eyes I can still see how the products line up.

I live and breathe toiletries in my windowless office.

The only mineral water offered is Naya, never Evian; Listerine must be produced in the US, not the UK; Kit-Kats must be made in the UK or the chocolate tastes different. The green-foiled aspirin hails from one certain Saudi Arabian factory.

Friends tell me that my letters to them arrive opened up and resealed, but they suppose that's 'normal for my job.' They keep saying dumb things on the phone: "Have you gone in the *Sheikh*'s private jet yet?" "Do any *Princesses* let you drive their Ferrari?" "Say hi to *Queen Money Bags* from me!!"—keywords that Justine tells me trips a listening device to record conversations. (I imagine the equipment is hidden beneath Mr. Malik's bed and operated by dexterous scorpions.)

Jacqui writes a lot of letters and since boundaries were never too great between us, in one she describes her new boyfriend's style of kissing. Most of that paragraph is blacked out by an anonymous censor's marker. We are monitored, this I know.

I can't make it to Helen my old roommate's wedding and nobody can understand why I have to work every day and can't fly in for it.

Mom sighs down the phone, "Jocelyn's in hospital again. They're trying some different anti-psychotics."

Jocelyn, who married tricky Burke, and had my oldest

niece when she was twenty-two, keeps having breakdowns.

"Oh my god, is she going to be okay?"

"Sure, sure," Mom soothes. "She just hasn't been eating right. If only she'd take the vitamin D that I get for her... Can I post you some?"

"No, Mom! They'll think that's drugs and it's the death penalty for that here."

Nobody in my family wants to say the word 'schizophrenia' about my beautiful, creative, big sister. It's as if that's a keyword that'll trip more than just phone lines being bugged. It'll cause a fundamental unraveling. The US$15,000 I've thrown at my parents so far hasn't miraculously fixed anyone. Siblings teeter on bankruptcy or heartache, slow healing or no healing. Jocelyn's last spectacular breakdown came after not eating any food for three solid weeks and talking non-stop to Jesus in the garden. It's as if my success allows some siblings to fall apart completely.

Rule #1: Don't talk about anything.

I wouldn't talk to anyone in my family as a sounding board or for guidance anyway. Not since I was little and they didn't seem to see me. It's much safer to hide myself away here in Xamnesia and grow a cashpot of money to keep myself (and somehow my family, although my sense of family is becoming untethered) *safe*.

In truth, I refuse to ask for advice because I cling to my status as 'the sorted out child.' I'm the one Mom never has had to worry about. I'm not giving that up for all the tea in China.

"But you're doing fine?" Mom winds up.

"Yeah, Mom. Great. I better go, got a call waiting. Love you."

"Take care, Liz," her voice crackles as we both hang up.

12

MOVEMENT 2

"Where are you now?"

"Hi, Captain… in my office."

"VIP say: All Laundry Go Home Bangkok. You go tell them."

I go to Laundry to see Thongchai and the guys. My laundry facilities are manned by a dozen Thai staff, all male, who handle items from a list of VIP properties. They're smiling guys with a love for getting any stain out of any fabric, leaving their eyes permanently red from the chemicals they handle fifty hours a week. Thongchai's in charge and deals exclusively with our key VIP's clothes. His rack divulges all sorts of secrets such as whether the VIP bothers with underwear. But I can't get into that. I could tell you if he wore briefs, but I'd have to kill you, remember?

All silk bed sheets are the domain of Soonchai—a large moon-faced man whose belly jiggles and who is found bent over the sheet press for hours at a time and otherwise sniffing a camphor-scented handkerchief.

"Hey guys…" I start.

"Morning, Miss Lizzie," they chorus, kindly reducing the volume on the music they blast from a transistor.

"I want to talk about problem with bed sheet, Miss," Thongchai says.

They know why I'm there.

One of the female VIPs is gunning for my Laundry staff because a set of white silk lingerie went to the wrong house yesterday (it was a mistress's knickers). That's why the female VIP wants all of these sweet kind people to lose their jobs.

The Thai staff are a spectrum of types. The waitresses are touchy-feely in a slightly calculating way, sharing their personal dramas and problems readily because they make me coffee. The maids are stoic, have seen *everything* and hope to get close to a VIP, not powerless Miss Lizzie. The chefs and stewards are aloof yet take everything to heart, tending towards addiction to the terrible mutant cousin of whisky that they drink here (which could make you blind if you drink it straight). But the laundry folk are sensual creatures, and the most promiscuous, for the sheer heck of it. Or maybe the chemicals they inhale all day play a part. It must be like sniffing glue or dropping Ecstasy. They are the free love crew. Thongchai runs his hand easily around my waist as he drags me off to talk. His hand is callous-free and he has the body of a Thai kick boxer with abdominals clearly rippling through his pristine T-shirt and soft chinos. Breathing droplets of fabric softener and inhaling steam has polished them all into smooth sex gods. But I'm here to save as many jobs as I can. Not notice any six-packs.

"VIP mad because Special Lady underwear go wrong property," I say. "What happen?"

Have I mentioned that I learned a new language? Pidgin English. It doesn't pay to use correct English grammar with the staff as it only obstructs communication.

"Soonchai he very tired, Miss. He work late shift one month now. But he happy go home Thailand. He go, everyone else stay."

"You want go home Thailand? But your family need many money," I argue.

Soonchai nods, smiling broadly.

All the staff has a village in Thailand each depending on their Xamnesian salary. Most need their money to pay for operations for extended family and have dreams of constructing a house. They all have children they see only two weeks per year. The lowliest is on US$250 per month. But that's 12,000 Thai Baht. A lot of Baht. I don't know one Thai staff member who doesn't have a sad story of what they fund with their salary. They never, ever voluntarily quit.

Thongchai answers, "He tired all the time because the hepatitis. So he happy go home. His brother now get job in Late Party kitchen so family okay."

"*Hepatitis*? Is it B or C?"

Thongchai smiles. Soonchai looks bashful as if I just

said he has an enormous member. When the Thai staff have no clue what I am on about, they bust out big grins, or start offering food.

"We have steam coconut egg bun. You want try, Miss Lizzie?" Soonchai asks.

"Not right now, thank you. Other staff has hepatitis?"

Thongchai nods, "Oh yes. Many. But it okay, Miss, we work hard for VIP family, can. No problem."

I don't know what to do, so I ring Justine, who takes off with this news like a crack journalist consulting with Mr. Malik and all sorts of higher-ups. Within hours, this news has spread... faster than Ebola. The private medical center concedes that no staff have been retested for communicable diseases since their arrival, however many years or months ago that is. (Even we were tested for HIV and other diseases in order to obtain our ID cards.) By noon I've inadvertently provoked mass blood screening for sexually transmitted diseases. Mr. Malik orders all 2,000-odd staff members to be retested.

There are dozens of hepatitis cases: B and C. And certain security guards who are very friendly with certain kitchen stewards test positive. A whole new terrain of activity reveals itself to me: the sex trade going on in Xamnesia is jaw-droppingly rampant. A maid has Hep C from going to the construction workers' campsites after dark and prostituting herself. The low paid make extra whatever way they can.

And one of my maids, Pinpet, tests HIV positive.

She's a quiet girl with acne scars, my age: twenty-four. I drive her to the medical center so a doctor can break the news. She's more excited about my car than the appointment, running her smooth fingers over the leather dashboard, limpid eyes boggling over the multi-stack CD-player stereo playing Radiohead's 'Creep' a little too loud because otherwise I'm going to cry.

We sit in the doctor's office and I keep trying not to cry because she doesn't even understand what the man is saying.

"In Thailand, you live with your family?" Doctor McGillacutty asks.

"No. I go to Bangkok from my village. Find husband. But he die. He very sick and die."

"When?"

"Before I come work for the VIPs. I very happy work for VIP family, Miss Lizzie…" she casts me a pleading look.

"We have to send you home," Doctor McGillacutty toys with his crystal paperweight and letter opener. "You are sick, Pinpet. You know about AIDS?"

She starts crying, "I can work very hard. Any house. You send me other house, Miss Lizzie, can? If VIP want me to go other house, I can?"

She's been a maid for seven months and always smiles even when I can see she's been given the short straw on shifts. We walk out with only my arm hugging around her waist for comfort. Which is no comfort at all.

Doctor McGillacutty shuts his door firmly.

There's no retesting for the positive cases, which makes me cringe when human error is so high around here and the makeshift blood-testing labs set up in our properties' canteens could cause easy mix-ups. One wrong sticker on a blood vial and that's a different name going home on the plane. And the treatment's universal: a one-way ticket home. Even for treatable Hep B sufferers, there is no healthcare offered. And no redundancy package. One month's wages in a slim brown envelope.

I return to House X with deflated Pinpet.

Captain appears in my office, followed by a waitress offering us coffee who chokes back audible sobs. The waitress isn't going, but all of the staff is in pieces about their friends being sacked, *just for being tired*, as they see it.

Rule #4: Don't tell anyone you're tired.

I shut my door softly once her footfalls fade.

"I already heard about Thongchai in Laundry. He stays," Captain starts.

"Okay… But shouldn't he take it easy? He's got C, not B. That's bad."

"It's taken five years to get a laundry guy the VIP likes to wash his clothes. Thongchai's happy to stay."

I tell him the rest of the results, he blanches, "Which waitress has Hep C?"

"Nim. She says it's a mistake. Can't we retest her?"

"Pretty? Looks like Nong?"

"Yeah…"

"I inform to Mr. Malik to tell the VIP," Captain says quickly.

"She swears she doesn't have anything."

"We'll say it's something else. Anemia or endometriosis."

I stare at him. "Why?"

But it dawns on me why. The VIP has been fooling around with that pretty waitress Nim…

"Don't think too much," Captain spins lightly on my guest office chair, swiveling and almost chortling. I could sock him.

"Sure."

He sighs. "I see you upset, Miss-Twenty-Four-Year-Old-Lizzie. But this is employment agency fault. It not safe for VIP family—imagine a waitress cut herself while she's serving the children?"

"Yeah, but the agency swears they were all tested before they came here."

Captain pouts in agreement, like this is all some giant fluky error on God's part.

"So they got infected while working *here*," I continue.

"There's a lot goes on between Thai staff," he shrugs. "They go with boyfriends, girlfriends, both at the same time… don't think too much, Miss Lizzie."

"And your security guard… go with male steward?" I add. "And VIPs can go with waitress?"

"Different culture, different view. Huge honor."

I open the door for him to leave. "Huge honor, is it?"

"Yes."

A few weeks after this bad bloodbath—when I can manage to sleep without images of Pinpet's limpid eyes flashing before me—I get kicked out of House X.

13

MOVEMENT 3

I must go see Mr. Malik at 10:00 a.m. This news alone should tell me I am toast. But I am optimistic, oblivious.

Mr. Malik has my résumé out when I reach his office. He laughs like a loon and a woman is draped over a settee. She has wavy red hair, a wavy smile, a wavy skinny body and wears way too much Shalimar perfume.

"Ah, Lizzie. This is Kristal. Kristal goes to X House now. You go to Y House. You drive her to X—show her everything—then Captain's people show you the way to Y. Don't think too much. Girl who think too much make big problem…" he taps the bugged-out veins on his temple, "*up here*. I'll see you."

That is the longest speech I've heard from him. With too much reassurance. This is bad.

"Who's at Y House?"

He mentions the VIP we figured Daisy works for. The young one who terminates people for looking at him sideways. And his mother and her sports team of adopted children.

"Why?" I stammer.

Mr. Malik wields my résumé, stabbing the last line, "You know cake. You help bakers with the motherfucking cakes—they need motherfucking cakes all week long. Orders from the mother."

As my 'Interests' at the bottom of my résumé I listed: 'Jogging, writing, and cake decorating.' Jogging is a distant memory and was to show I'm not some pothead couch potato. Writing was to casually let them know I planned on working on my novel in my free time (which hasn't happened once yet). Cake decorating was to show I have *a sense of humor*. Mr. Malik cannot be serious. I did cake decorating for compulsory 'sport' one semester of middle grade school because I am so uncoordinated. It was cake decorating for twelve year olds, not even high school level!

However, my mind clings to two words: the mother. Maybe I'll get along better with somebody's mother.

"The mother is there?" I ask.

"Yes, very nice lady. She take care of many people. *Never be seen by her or she'll sack you.* That's all."

So I won't be getting along with anybody's mother.

I drive Kristal to X House. She smokes without bothering to roll the window down. Her fingernails are bitten down to the quick. She'll be less cocky after six weeks in this simmering Crock-Pot of paranoia and protocol. Maybe. She's pretty cocky.

"Did you hear you'll be living at my place?" she says.

"What?"

"Scottie said one of you three needs to move downstairs because I have the whole third floor, and he picked you in case I need to ask you stuff about X House. But I severely doubt I'll have to ask you anything. I've already moved into the pink room."

First she takes my House and now I have to live with her? I swallow hard.

"So, what were you doing to get the job?"

"I'm an actress. TV commercials mainly, but you know."

"Right. And you're from…?"

"Cape Town."

At least she hasn't twigged yet that in Xamnesia the best answer is a non-answer. I don't bother to enlighten her.

When we arrive at the staff parking lot, a silver Mercedes is outside. Just-off-the-container-ship new.

"That'll be my car," Kristal declares. "Scottie promised me a Merc. Let's see my house then."

I think I hate her. Normally I'm so keen to make new friends but this girl makes me want to trip her up as she walks into House X and turns up the charm on *my* security guards and maids.

All I have is a simmering hope that she'll irrevocably offend someone and be on a plane back to Cape Town. I compose myself into Teflon-coated Zen. When the waitresses hug me good-bye I am the most extrovert I've been. Captain shakes my hand.

"I'm sorry for your transfer, but we all work for the same VIP. Different property, same protocol."

I look at him. Did he put in a bad word about me, to turf me out? No, I decide. He's all about stability. Doing the job.

"Thanks for all your advice, Captain. Who's the Captain at Y House?" I ask.

He doesn't hoot or chortle. Bad, bad sign.

As I snake around the back roads, following a driver and wiping away a tear, Justine rings.

"Lizzie! I've just heard about your move to Y House! This is awfulawfulawful. I'm soooooo sorry for you."

"Thanks."

"What's Kristal's number? I need to talk to her."

Obviously now that I'm no longer at X, Justine hones in on the new girl. Go right ahead.

I can't ring Charlotte for a pep talk—she has President Clinton visiting for seventy-two hours. I ring Idora.

"You can do it, hon. Just be yourself."

After the call, I bite my lip. Who is 'myself'? Again, I'm not sure of my reference point for who Lizzie is. Lizzie changed her name the second she landed here. She hasn't rung her Mom in three weeks. She writes letters and faxes that say nothing and hasn't even peeked at the novel-in-progress. She *took up smoking*!

The back-of-house area is all gray concrete—the ugly foundation to the pretty VIP areas on the flip side.

Staff swarm like bees, some load trays of food onto golf carts to whiz up the service driveway, others pull racks of silk frocks on velvet hangers. Total chaos. The white uniforms and frenetic activity remind me of a mental asylum.

I say some hellos, start up the metal stairs; a dozen pairs of eyes tracking my progress. "Miss Lizzie, you want sandwich for lunch?" a young cook asks.

"Maybe later." Not only do they know my name but also what the last cooks have been making me for lunch. Staff spreads news faster here than Reuters.

I'd like to say I had a warm welcome with smiles from all of the security personnel who were consummate professionals. But that didn't happen. Y House was about the worst property in Xamnesia: full of long-long-long term employees of the VIPs who viewed newcomers with suspicion and mistrust. They made Captain at House X look like my fairy godfather.

Time is last seen sinking into quicksand wearing concrete flip-flops. Glug-glug. I am physically present at House Y from 9.30 a.m. until 11.45 p.m. seven days a week and yet I feel as if I do nothing all day. Time loops in a déjà-vu of orders from nannies and butlers and paid friends and Mr. Malik, dissolving into talk sessions with Charlotte and Idora. Every shrill of my cell phone makes my pulse race with the eternally rude opening line: "Where are you now?"

Time is no longer mine. Sleep is owned by anyone with my number.

I have dreams I am on Mars. On the moon. Back at Toto Restaurant, waitressing as I waitressed when I met Scottie and he gave me this 'dream' job. I throw down the plates at Toto because I realize my job in Xamnesia is in jeopardy and I am late, late for a very important date. Can't find the right tunnel to fall down and shoot me back out here. I can taste the Stoli vodka and the splash of fresh lemon juice in my drink. I find a phone book and the number for Xamnesia Airlines is 151515151515151515. My room service bill is $5350 yet I ordered nothing. I drive and run out of gas. My hands don't work; they are toy hands.

All signs of work-related stress.

Just as the weeks blur into miasma, so does the climate. Darkness swallows the yellow day yet the heat never recedes. It squats between 85-102°F. The seasons reduce to arid and slightly less arid: apparently there is a rainy season for one week in November. The climate sucks all energy out of you and gives you the squirms.

I tug out my eyelashes to make a wish upon.

It's always the same: 'Please, make me some nice VIP's personal assistant so I can escape Xamnesia on trips.'

Daisy goes on trips. She's on the passenger manifest and gets extra envelopes every time she hops on the private plane. Justine's started traveling too, she went with someone on a super yacht up to the Suez Canal last week. If only *someone* would give me that chance, then I'd do the *best job ever* because sticking around Y House is turning me psycho.

Nobody can see that I am losing the plot. I am a walking sham, a chameleon who changes her skin for everyone she tries to impress.

The high from the Envelope has long gone. I'm a spinning wheel in mud. What gets to me is the feeling of VIPs watching me scurry around the property from their mirrored windows.

SEAL comes to town for a birthday concert. Backstage, he actually chats up Charlotte, but we can't figure out how to access him beyond that. He's staying at one of Justine's guesthouses and it's not as if Justine would invite us round there to hang out. Charlotte does, however, suss out the address of Ringo, the audio-visual technician in charge of the concerts here. Ringo's the key to a social life beyond our four walls at Seven Storey White Building.

Idora spends 100 hours a week inside her property. She talks less, is addicted to these sweet buns with sticky insides like squashed flies. She's less sharp. Her bob grows out raggedly. She had to buy a load of cream shirts and white bras and camisoles to wear because her all-black wardrobe was too much for her property's reproving security minders. Mention dancing, ballet or her studio aspirations and she frowns like you're speaking in tongues.

"I don't have enough saved up yet," she says vaguely.

Charlotte has sultans, emirs, kings and the odd president staying at her mini-palace for two days out of each month and otherwise she is bored to tears. Her only excitement is when the gardeners capture snakes (that they take home to eat) or chase dromedaries off the property's immense back lawn. She takes up running at the gym—where she crosses paths with Daisy who never seems busy except to jump on the private plane—and regales us with stories of Daisy yakking up in the toilets.

Charlotte slips out for drinks with Ringo and his crew, discreet audio-visual techies from all over: Chicago to Glasgow. With his Bon Jovi hair, love of ACDC T-shirts, endless supply of spirits and beer, and under-the-radar parties, Ringo is the leader of his very own 'Drink Club' and rule #1 is: *You do not talk about Drink Club*. But I always seem to get home too late to join Charlotte on her merry escapades.

Kristal, who I'm forced to cohabitate with, says she's twenty-five, but I see her passport one day and she's a lying twenty-nine. But of course I get along with her. I get along with everyone, remember? We play a lot of backgammon and drink Red Bull mixed with Hennessy XO cognac because we have nothing else to drink. I have a feeling she's heading for an early check-out from Hotel Xamnesia. She still has too much confidence. People with confidence don't last here.

It doesn't occur to me to get happy with my own

company and take up yoga or meditation or any such thing. I buy a Toshiba laptop to work on my novel but it's hard to sustain concentration. I don't try to get an Internet connection. The telephone's not even in our names. Daisy hints that requesting the Internet was part of what got Hannah the boot.

I sign up for language lessons to learn diphthong-heavy Xamnesian, but drop out after the third class is again interrupted by phone calls with orders, reprimands, and unintelligible barking. When I spend time on my own, more eyelashes end up yanked out. My eyes are desolate. Just like my love life. Except that's about to change.

14

MEN 2

House Y has this diminishing effect on not just me. Everyone's a paper doll of themselves, shuffling around on auto pilot as if our Mister Coffees are spiked with Thorazine or Respiradol. The jokes we tell are G-rated jokes. We dress not to cause offence. The paid friends play sports just hard enough to work our VIP, but never wind him. It's no surprise there are no All Blacks playing rugby here—nobody could be paid enough to tackle our VIP to the ground.

Sports celebrities and friends arrive and leave like tours of duty. Personal lives are left back at the hotel room.

Of course, in any workplace people do not wail about their private lives—but it's all warped—it's our workplace but not the VIP's workplace, it's their lives. When there's no let up to the editing yourself of your real reactions for long periods people really do end up emotionless shells.

Everyone seems poisoned by 'easy' money, which

really isn't 'easy' because it sucks our souls out through our eyelids at night when we aren't looking. And every teaspoon of soul that goes doesn't replenish naturally.

There's one paid friend I keep noticing. Carlton. Carlton is another friend of our VIP's from the Swiss school they all attended and an actor, or wants to be, back in LA. Out here, he's Carlton the joker. Carlton the rather beautiful. Carlton has a little bit of an attitude. I can see he's bored out of his tree. He's been in Xamnesia just long enough to get a black Mercedes station wagon worth US$25,000 for his birthday and to become so bored he chats to me.

It's not like the friends have a hard life—they get US$30,000 per month to watch TV and play on our VIP's team. But Carlton has a sense of individualism that's too high for him to cope here.

He gives me a wry, 'what-can-I-say' smile and is always the last of the friends to leave the Sports Complex at the end of the working day. I read this as keen interest in *moi*, bordering on true love.

He smokes Marlboro Lights like me so that's an excuse to ring him one dry night, and drive to the Sheraton to lend him some, and look at him suggestively and end up on his double bed with its ghastly, floral bedspread. The next morning the worst thing is sneaking out of the Sheraton without running into (you can go ahead and insert a laundry list of sports celebs here) or any of the other paid schoolchums living in the Sheraton.

When I leave I realize I put my lenses in the wrong way around and drive back to Seven Story White Building squinting into the rising sun.

Anyone with half a brain would realize that night at the Sheraton is as far as it's going with Carlton the Hollywood Actor. I, however, have only one-eighth of a brain by now, so I attempt to turn this into a long-term *thing*. His nervous indifference around me only flames my interest. I strike up conversation only to strike out. He edges away from my spot on the wall where I hang out near the buffet, out of view of our sporty VIP and the VIP mother when she turns up.

Two weeks later, Charlotte and I get wind of an after-midnight party at Nick's, my VIP's number one paid buddy.

Nick lives down 'Street 334,' a road behind the main road where a lot of big-wigs live. At the top of the road the male Thai staff are housed in a crumbling apartment block with plumbing issues and dangerous electricity. The area teems with people who should not see my license plate out so late. I park 100 meters from Nick's McMansion, practically in a bush.

It's a quiet party. A mere fifty entourage mill about, drinking tequila at the bar and lazing in the pool. We walk past Miguel, a Spanish-Jordanian go-to guy, who models himself on Mr. Malik, hollering into his phone: "Only the strong will survive! The rest we spit on from above! *Fuck* them!!! *Fuck* them!!!"

"Can I do anything to help?" I ask as he hangs up in rage. I ask all the entourage if there's anything I can do to help. This is my strategy to get onside with them and eventually onto a private plane to carry shopping bags or *something*.

"My mother," he sniffs, pocketing his phone. "She's upset that I will miss her seventieth birthday."

If you haven't seriously upset your family by missing key events—birthdays, heart surgery, funerals—then you're not doing your job well enough here.

Charlotte makes a dozen new friends instantly and I slowly circle the room, edging closer to Carlton, who hasn't given me any more than a casual wave and an echo of Nick's, "Y'allright?"

Time falls into the swimming pool and comes up gasping at four-thirty in the morning, when Carlton starts kissing one of the mother's beauticians in full view. I watch, my poise puddling on the marble tiles as he paws at her tight sexy body, and I realize how unenthusiastic he was the other night when I lent him cigarettes and my big-booty, B-cup body. Miguel wolf-whistles. Nick whoops, "Take a room." They reach third base on the marble tiles.

"Let's go," Charlotte herds me out.

We don't say good-bye. It's pitch black with no streetlights. I'm driving drunk but don't care. I've driven drunk in Xamnesia, and in New Zealand, nothing can touch me. I'm invisible and invincible. I start down Street 334, but it starts to rain. Crack, flash and then no way I can see the road. This is the one week of rainy season! I pull over and turn off the engine, avoiding the mawing pit of a storm drain, which I now understand why they exist. Tequila makes my heart race above the roar of the biblical deluge.

"Babe, Carlton's a loser dickhead waster with no talent and no taste," Charlotte pronounces. She is a sweetheart for bolstering me but I know it's going to do no good.

"I know."

"Don't feel bad about it. Don't give him another second of your thoughts, Lizziegirl. You're worth way *way* more," she continues.

"Sure."

"You'll go on to bigger and better things than he ever will. Mark my words," she insists.

"Yeah. Right." I don't believe a word. I am a zero. An invisible, shameful zero of a girl.

The rain stops. God-turned-off-a-tap sudden. I'm so tired I can barely lift my arms to turn the ignition. The BMW whines and won't start.

I try again, then again, then again. I've gone and flooded the engine.

"We are a bit fucked," Charlotte admits.

I slap the steering wheel, hyperventilating in panic: without a car I really *am* a zero and oh no! I'm parked right opposite the male Thai staff housing and in an hour the sun will be up and my car will be seen by everyone and even Mr. Malik drives past here in the mornings and how can I resuscitate my car and get us the hell out of here?

"Let's go back and pray someone there's sober," Charlotte yabbers.

We start walking back to Nick's—the sole option. A white 4x4 Kijang appears out of the pre-dawn gloom. A local guy rolls down his window. He smiles like it's absolutely normal to find two Western girls, drunk on Street 334 in the dark, with a dead car. Maybe it is.

"You need help?"

"Yes!"

"The engine flooded."

He leaps out of his jeep and slides behind the wheel. Gives it a go. Which only floods it more.

"I can drive you, where you want to go?"

"If you can take us to our apartment near the airport? We can come back in my car and by then yours'll be fine," Charlotte figures.

He nods, gesturing to the back seat.

"Thank you!" we sing.

Charlotte and I climb in. He has a large sack or something across the backseat and another taking up the passenger seat. But it's too dark to make out what's in the sack and I don't care—as long as he's not an ax murderer I don't care about anything. Charlotte explains directions, leaning on the sack to be heard. I lean against the other side of the sack and close my eyes.

After ten minutes, the sack has made my torso and arm all cold—*and wet*—and when I examine it, with the light of dawn brightening everything inside the Kijang, I see it isn't a sack at all.

It's a frozen skinned carcass.

Goat. Defrosting skinned goat. With black defrosting eyes and pink defrosting lips pulled back over yellow defrosting teeth. I recoil. Charlotte recoils. Our shirts are *soaked pink* from defrosting bloodied goat.

In that moment, Charlotte turns vegetarian and I turn off eating altogether.

"Ah, you meet my friend," our chauffeur laughs. "I take him to sell in the market."

I melt into the wallpaper. Barely speak. Regret my attempt to socialize with these people. I ask if I can help with things but I know the entourage will never accept me. I don't go anywhere that any House Y people will be. I stay at home.

Carlton returns to LA having sold his birthday present Mercedes for a mere US$10,000. I say, "Good luck, Carlton, I'm sure you'll make it big with your acting."

He doesn't.

15

MISCHIEF 2

Joy of joys! We are handed 10,000 *drachmas* each and plane tickets to take ourselves shopping in Dubai!

The last six months have felt like I've been locked in a padded room with one-million-piece puzzle to do—whenever I looked up and thought my God, I'm still doing this?—there was no echo from the outside world to indicate I should do anything else so I put my head down again, fixated on getting another piece to fit.

The catch is, we can't go to Dubai all together. I have to go with Justine. Idora and Charlotte can go together. Daisy's traveled so much she doesn't need to add to her five racks of suits. Kristal recently arrived so doesn't need the break. I'm forlorn not to go with Idora and Charlotte. I'm not a huge fan of Justine's sheer enthusiasm. She is such a goody two shoes I must watch myself around her. But, as soon as we're airborne with our phones switched off, Justine transforms into Miss Mischief. Gone is all her sermonizing about the correct way to pour mango juice at the dull functions. All Daisyisms dry up.

Justine snakes her arm through mine as we march through customs with nobody giving us a hard time. The air's hot, but not as suffocating as Xamnesia's yellow air. We hit the luxurious malls.

"Oooh, you have to try this on!" Justine says.

"That's a ridiculous top. You have to get it," she encourages.

"I've *got* to buy underwear—there isn't a bra that fits me in 'the Desert,'" she declares.

I think I'm supposed to spend my ten thousand on suits for work so I linger in Emporio Armani (not Giorgio) and DKNY. The practical gal's brands. I don't see any reason to buy underwear because no guy's appreciating me in a thong.

When Justine's finished buying up La Perla, she's somehow acquired a guy, carrying her bags. He's hale, tanned, with crinkly puppy-dog eyes.

"This is Ryan," she steers me around a rack of Issy Miyake perfumes, feigning rubbing the scent on my wrists as if she's marking me as her territory. "Please, Lizzie, you can't tell anyone. Promise?"

"Sure… it's none of my business. I didn't know you had a boyfriend."

"I broke up with him when I went to Xamnesia. But he still wants to be friends."

"Sure," I reply. I'm not interested in stabbing anyone in the back. Xamnesia's way too small for that. It's lifeboat small, in fact. I'm pretty sure if I tried to bring

Justine down, she'd find a way to bring me down with her.

Hhmm, but it sure doesn't look like Ryan just wants to be friends. We go to dinner—he handfeeds her sushi. We down shots at the Hard Rock Café—he's suddenly got her on his lap. If you down twenty-four shooters at the Hard Rock Café, they give you the shot glasses. I only manage to do half that before Justine urges that we call it a night.

The next day, Justine and Ryan are not seen for breakfast. Or lunch. At three in the afternoon, I timidly knock on her hotel door. Our flight's at six.

"We were just about to call you," she says, buttoning her blouse. He's stuffing himself into jeans. I lean against the doorway. A surliness radiates from me—which I explain as a hangover. Justine is lucky I'm a nice person and not a Daisy. And why didn't I think to get a guy to fly up to hang out with me? I should have gotten Solomon, the guy I fax flirtatious correspondence with, to fly here—a guy I never did anything with in Auckland, but who sweetly professed his love for me the night before I left and who immediately became more desirable as soon as I was 12,000 miles away. He said he posted me an intriguing birthday present involving vodka, but the customs agents confiscated it.

We go through duty-free, a wary silence between us. Justine buys me yards of cerise silk to get sewn into a Cheong-sum. I let her buy me that and perfume. I don't get her anything. On the flight home, she's exhausted, but she doesn't sleep. She tells me all about her life—how her dad's really hard on her, nothing's ever good enough for him, how he expects her to be a huge success, how her kid sister has learning difficulties, how she sends a lot of the money she's made to help her sister.

"Doesn't your dad have the money to help her?" I toy with the shitty roasted peanuts and my plastic tumbler of spiced tomato juice. I'm filled with reluctance to land back in Xamnesia. It was too short. I spent the time unwisely. I want a do-over.

"Dad doesn't believe in the alternative therapies that my mom and I think work. Ryan keeps an eye on my sister."

"Sounds hard, having a dad like that."

"I'm so glad I got to go with you, Lizzie. Get to talk properly. You're such an amazing person," she squeezes my cold hand and I feel like I used to feel when I'd drive everyone home—like the useful chauffeur they could trust. Trust makes me feel worthy.

When I go to the airport to pick up Idora and Charlotte from their shopping trip, I feel a pang watching them weave their way through customs beyond the glass doors —they wear long dark dresses made of silk and lace— practically see through, they're still drunk, laughing their heads off, are almost hauled off somewhere by the custom's agent. They launch through the doors to hug me, their breath champagne-scented, laughing their heads off. They took their own bottle of champagne on the flight to drink. They had way more fun than I did. I feel destined to miss out on the best fun. All my life I'm watching shinier, happier, more confident gals doing it better, getting their heart's desire while I'm too sluggish and dull to assert myself. My mom's attitude to assertiveness pops into my mind: a dark art practiced by vamps and mean girls. All my childhood she implored us to be *good*. Never strong.

At Seven Story White Building the girls parade a startling array of cool clothes and make-up. I show them my haul, which now looks like stuff Daisy would wear.

Unfortunately, Charlotte lost her phone in a bar and Mr. Malik gave her a telling off for it. "Like being flayed alive," Charlotte says ruefully.

"How was Lean Justine?" they ask.

"Trying to get me on her side—for some unknown reason—I think she's lonelier here than she lets on. She says Daisy's quite unpleasant to hang out with."

I don't betray Justine's confidence. Is this me being a good friend or a spineless sap?

"Ha," Charlotte scoffs, "so she says."

They brought me a white silk dressing gown for being so brave about going with Justine. I share the shot glasses that Hard Rock Café gave me (because I did manage to finish the twenty-four shooters after Justine and Ryan left the bar to have sex).

New Year's Eve and we're back at the scene of our

crimes against Xamnesia concerts—the Playground—where Michael Jackson performs for the country.

On stage he's incredible. His choreography is poetry. He dances like a robot genetically-spliced with a fairy. He is truly the King of Pop. When he thanks the VIPs and tells us he loves Xamnesia I believe him. I figure he must be incredible in real life. But when he appears the next day at House Y's Sport Complex, I am again struck by how my imagination misses reality by a mile.

He shuffles down the gray stairs to greet the VIPs. A bony lanky husk in his military black jacket with the white stripes, the white socks and tight black pants and black loafers. He barely speaks and when he does it's in a whisper. He looks traumatized, terrified of people. Michael Jackson makes these reclusive VIPs look like talk show hosts.

He has a bodyguard the size of a public toilet, who protects him while he signs a million photos and smiles for the camera. The music producer who sets up the concert spots me on the sideline.

"You want a photo with our man?" he says.

"No, no, don't go to any trouble," I say. I feel sick. This is because last night after the concert (which ended at quarter to midnight), after the fireworks back at House Y on the terrace (requiring catering yet nobody appeared to eat anything), I joined Charlotte and Idora who were partying with Michael Jackson's better-looking roadies (Charlotte found them, I didn't ask how) and we drank until five o'clock this morning, snogging the roadies. Them not talking about their boss, us not divulging details about our bosses. (Although we did hear that MJ has laryngitis so the concert was entirely lip-synched.)

I look like the Wreck of the Hesperus, as my Mom says. That was a shipwreck where a young girl was found drowned after being tied to the mast by her father, the captain. Longfellow's poem and now an expression for looking so scruffy you are unrecognizable to humanity.

"He won't bite," the agent drags me across the Sports Complex.

Our sullen VIP's nostrils flare slightly, maybe smelling vodka ooze from my pores, maybe thinking, 'Who in the hell *is* that?'

I'm frogmarched up to Michael Jackson.

"This is Lizzie, the best property manager in Xamnesia. She'd love a photo with you."

Michael Jackson looks at me with mute pain. He's so incredibly white his face is a chalky mille-feuille. Whiter than me. Or, perhaps not—today I am alabaster. I swallow so I'm not sick on anybody.

"May I go to the washroom first, please?" It's the first full sentence he's said. He begs for this loo break with such fear of failing to live up to expectations in his falsetto voice that I want to give him a huge hug, but he'd break into a million pieces if I did. You poor man! Or boy. Or whatever you are!

"Of course you can!" I gush, indicating to the bodyguard the route to the Guest Toilet so he can escort Michael. Then I stress that I should have indicated the VIP Toilet. I'm an idiot. How bad are his phobias these days? He's in there a long time. There is someone in this world whose self-effacement, whose wish for invisibility exceeds mine.

Michael Jackson was born in the same year as Madonna, Prince, and my unwell genius sister, Jocelyn. It was Year of the Dog.

Jocelyn was the one who spent infinite amounts of time with us little kids, wrote plays for us to act, dressed us up, she's the only one who took photos *just of me* (otherwise I am a blurry grin in the background or one of many in group shots), she painted our portraits in oil. She had her first breakdown when she was twenty-six. There's the before-Jocelyn and now the after-Jocelyn. She reviles the label schizophrenic, who wouldn't? She's not violent in the slightest and sadly her condition is plagued with stereotypes of aggressive hallucinogenic misfits. Okay, she does constantly hear messages from Jesus Christ, and since I came to Xamnesia to work for VIPs she's convinced the British royal family are trying to kill Dad. She says Queen Elizabeth II is in on the murder of one million girlfriends but she's 'covering' it. To 'cover it' in this altered context is to pray and pray and pray to block psychic harm directed at people. It keeps poor Jocelyn up all night. She lives off coffee and potato chips.

The agent gets his photo of us. Wrecked alabaster Lizzie with Michael Jackson hugging me around my waist as if we are family.

It shocks me that he's willing to hug me. Is his arm his real arm? Or the arm that takes over when he's told to do something? Is he functioning like a star that loves his fans because that's what's been beaten into him all his life? Or is this how he really is? How can he look so terrified of people and then grip them so tight?

His arm is a scarecrow's twig. But for that moment of his left arm around me he infuses me with... something other-worldly. *Michael Jackson is hugging me.* Am I huggable?

I don't tell Justine that MJ hugged me. I want to keep the otherworldly feeling of self-worth that his arm squeezed into me. When I think of him and consider my big sister, Jocelyn, who is so gifted and amazing (and who knows, what if she's right that the British royal family is murdering people?), it makes terrible sense to me that in order to shine, be a creative genius, to hear the message, we might also be reduced to a husk of a human.

16

MONEY 2

I meet up with Charlotte and Idora at 'Aisha the Tailor's' shop (in other words her lounge) to be fitted for traditional silk outfits for the upcoming national celebrations to mark the end of Ramadan, fasting month.

There are two types of traditional dress: the *xamalama*—a.k.a. the silk potato sack—a loose boxy top with shoulder pads circa 1985 falling to mid-thigh, over a straight ankle-length skirt; and the sexy *zozolama*—a figure-hugging long top with plunging neckline and buttons from breast to navel, over a leg-skimming long skirt with a split up the back to the knee. Neither is a get-up you can run in. You mince instead, slowly.

We've been instructed to wear the frumpy *xamalama* variety. No surprise there.

Aisha, with insistent fingers, showed me many silk swathes a few weeks ago. I chose the plainest thing I could find: red, blue, and purple backgrounds with a 'Versace-inspired' pattern of yellow safety pins and coins. Hideous.

I told Aisha to cut generously; I look like something a cashed-up ogre would blow his nose on. But I don't care. The frumpier the better. Swanning around in the sexy *zozolama* get-up would be like mooning my tetchy VIP's mama.

The other girls have the same level of bagginess going on. Then Justine pulls in, dashing inside, tearing off her clothes, yabbering she doesn't have much time and must have her final fitting pronto.

We're offered iced teas while we wait—these silk handkerchiefs are setting us back about US$500 each.

I notice Justine's *xamalama* are cut close. The skirts are so tight you can read the washing instructions on her underpants

"Are you sure that's going to be okay? It's not exactly a sack on you," I ask.

Justine runs her hands up and down herself. "The VIPs want us to look good."

"Who told you that?" Charlotte asks.

"A little birdie."

Charlotte raises her eyebrows.

"Was it Mr. Malik who told you?" Idora asks, just to see if she'll tell the truth or not.

Justine peels off her last *xamalama* without replying, pausing in her ridiculously lacy bra and briefs in a sickly shade of lemon, before slowly wriggling into her long microfiber dress.

The question goes unanswered. "Is Kristal getting some *xamalama* made up?" Justine asks Aisha. "You know Kristal: tall, but has a problem…"

Justine mimes sweat under the armpits.

"Ah, very tall, beautiful like Cindy Crawford? She order *zozolama*," Aisha shrugs.

"She's asking for it. It's really bad that you share an apartment with her, Lizzie. You don't want to get into trouble by association."

"I don't associate with her. Anyway, she says she takes her instructions from Mr. Malik…"

"Pfft… he doesn't even like her!"

Who knows what to believe.

I ask Kristal about her traditional silk situation.

She scoffs, "Mr. Malik told me to look good, so I'm going to look good. Justine can suck my dick."

Kristal has not dialed down her personality for this place, not one notch.

She shows me her beauties. Lilac, gold, ivory and burgundy *zozolama* so tight they're like cling wrap on her model's body. Holy moly. This is shaping up to be a showdown. Clash of the colorful. *Xamalama* vs. *zozolama*. Last silk standing wins.

The morning of the celebrations, there is another knock on the door at 7:00 a.m. It's the same nameless guy with the cash. He hands each of us an Envelope and white cardboard box, snickering at Kristal's La Prairie facemask and my Strawberry Shortcake slippers.

I go open my goodies in my bathroom. Inside the box

is a diamond ring with two white-gold bangles. In my envelope is $30,000 *drachma*s (US$15,000).

Wee-hee, I exhale long and slow.

Seeing a wallop of cash again brings an instant high and low in one. High that I've been given such wealth—me!—unworthy slip of a geek from a big family of kooks with lack up to our eyeballs.

And then the Low: my traitorous thoughts of quitting Xamnesia must be quashed, I can't quit now, the VIPs' generosity has ensured another lap round the track, I can't quit on this family who are so generous to me—me! a little nobody squirmy, unworthy… you get the picture. A lot of negative self-talk swirls around and around.

Kristal stomps around muttering that *ten thousand drachma* is a measly tip to these guys.

I'm shocked and say nothing—my tip's three times more than Kristal's?

I hide my envelope in my waistband until I can deposit it. She demands to see my ring and studies them both, squinting at them out on the terrace, finally pronouncing her diamond to be slightly bigger.

Later, Justine rings to tell me the stones are 'one carat' and E-rated meaning they're virtually flawless. I don't even ask her how she knows this stuff. She will be right. She wants to know if Kristal got an envelope.

"Uh, I didn't see exactly," I waffle.

"But she's wearing *zozolama*?"

"Yeah."

"I told you. She's trouble. But don't worry, Lizzie, I

tell everyone how sweet you are so they don't associate you with that stupid woman."

"Thanks, Justine."

Idora's phone rings and she steps out of the Thai Café cursing, "They can't even blow their nose without me!" She is utterly indispensable at her property because the chief property manager—a woman who's worked for the family for eight years—just ran away with one million dollars in petty cash.

Charlotte, Idora and I have taken to meeting for lunch at the Thai Café—where we munch through red and green curries, slurp thick milky coffees, and smoke.

Whenever Justine arrives, the mood shifts and I find myself shutting up—not keen to upset Justine who seems to be looking out for me, but also not wanting to look too friendly with her to skeptical Charlotte and Idora.

But Justine's not here today so I divulge all about Kristal and Justine's impending survival of the silkiest mortal combat.

"Don't get caught up in it, Lizziegirl," Charlotte shrugs pushing aside her unfinished curry.

Charlotte's a bit depressed. She hasn't had many visits lately. She is going 'fucking bananas,' in her words. I can tell she finds my unspoken friendliness with Justine unpalatable. It's only because there are so few of us here.

I 'standby' in House Y's Sports Complex, in my baggy potato sacks. The buffet heaves with special dishes to celebrate. And cake. Mountainous cakes I've been supervising the decorating of. You've never seen cakes like these: three feet squared behemoths of sugary lard and plastic supporting apparatus. Themed wonders in flavors such as black bean, mango, litchi. Whatever happened to good ol' Betty Crocker Devil's Food Cake?

The paid friends jibe me about my *xamalama*: "What's with the parachute?" "Did you walk through a clothes line on your way in, Lizzie?" "Gone local on us, have you?" Ha, ha. So funny.

After three days of seeing Kristal swing through the door, her *zozolama* looking more and more wilted, I figure Justine is winning. Kristal drinks a large Chivas Regal every night on the terrace and shouts at the camels to fuck off.

And the day after the celebrations end, I walk in the door at midnight to find Kristal, livid, no longer scribbling or shouting, just crying, with none-other-than Scottie patting her hand and freely pouring Laphroig.

"I only got one fucking tip of 10,000 *drachma* the whole four months I've been here, Scottie! I didn't even get to go shopping in Dubai! All I've made is my salary, that's sweet fuck-all. I want Mr. Malik to pay me out!!! I've *seen things*!"

"There, there, pal," Scottie looks alarmed. "Lizzie, how's it going? I hear you're taking care of the mother. Well done."

I don't bother to set him right on how much of a

fantasy that job description is. I'm suddenly sad for Kristal.

"What happened?"

But it's clear what happened. Her outfit caused offence. It's Go Home Cape Town for Miss Kristal.

"Scottie, get me more money!"

"I'll see what I can do, pal…" he sprints for the door. "I'll try to reach Mr. Malik."

"He's useless. Talk to the fucking key VIP!"

Kristal's on a plane within two days. Employment visa canceled. Identity card revoked. I don't know if she manages to negotiate a redundancy package, but she's cheery, if a little inebriated, for her departure—in Business Class. And she lets it slip that all along her salary was five times' what the rest of us are on.

There's nobody to play backgammon with.

I'm not reinstated at House X.

Justine gets House X.

I continue to rot at horrid Y.

17

CRASH 1

Idora is transferred to London. She's not told how long she'll be there so she packs everything. Charlotte and I are distraught, and thrilled, and envious.

"Why don't they give me a busier place than my marble mausoleum?" Charlotte laments, sucking on a cigarette.

"I'd trade you for House Hell," I offer.

"At least you see people."

"Paid people. And evil nannies."

"Only one thing for it, Lizziegirl," she says, stirring and going for her phone, to ring up Ringo. Ringo's the only one we can trust to go shake off our down moods with. Ringo and his inflatable alligator in his pool. I christen the alligator, Bolster, and I tell him all of my secret hopes: that Xamnesia is making me a better, stronger character when I fear it's doing the opposite.

At the end of June 1997, a month before our first year's contract expires; we wake up to a letter slipped under our apartment doors. We've heard about the Letter Under the Door. It will say if our contract is being renewed for another year, or not. 'Not' means we leave within two days. To anyone reading this who employs people can I just say that this has to be the classiest way of informing your staff of their worth to you?

Justine got her Letter three weeks ago because she started in Xamnesia ahead of us (always ahead, that lithe Justine)—she was renewed. Charlotte and I get ours on a Saturday morning. I go upstairs to Charlotte's and knock on the door timidly with mine unopened. Charlotte spies hers on the floor and tears into it.

Without a word, she goes out onto the terrace and lights a cigarette.

Charlotte is not renewed. I am. Charlotte doesn't want to talk about it. I go back downstairs.

Justine rings me twenty minutes later.

"Did you get your Letter, Lizzie?"

"I did. Charlotte's contract isn't renewed. Know any reason for that?"

"Oooh! That's too bad. She's a sweetheart."

"But she hasn't done anything wrong! Can't you maybe talk to… someone…?"

"She must have gone to some illegal party. Or drunk alcohol…"

"But you had Ryan meet you in…"

"He's my friend," she interrupts swiftly. "There's nothing *I can do*. I'm not a VIP, am I? Charlotte was bored and let everyone know it."

I swallow. Sure, Charlotte's been to more parties at Ringo's than we've had home-cooked meals. (Literally. We have appliances such as rice cookers still embalmed in polystyrene.) But Justine's mischief with Ryan doesn't affect her because neither Charlotte nor I have any proximity to those in power. We can't mention anything into the right-hand guys' ears.

"Can we talk to Scottie?"

Charlotte is packing her CDs and bangles. She's philosophical. Relieved, even. "I don't care, doll. I'd rather leave. This place is doing my nut in. This is all people like Justine's doing."

"It must be because we're bugged…"

"We're not bugged! As if the VIPs sit around reading reports on us going to lame-ass parties. It's the people around the VIPs that poison opinion. Justine's always out to score points. What do you think she talks to Mr. Malik about at X House? How sweet you and I are? When she says, *sweet*, she means, *naïve idiot*. She'd play her own grandmother like a two-bit banjo."

I am sick to my stomach. With Charlotte gone and Idora transferred to London, my thread of reason and sanity flies off with them. My pack's broken up like an ice flow that drifted too far from Antarctica.

"There's a beach party tonight. I'll drive. No need to hide my license plate now."

We arrive at the unnamed beach a little after midnight. The air's dank and briny. Ringo's rigged up a stereo system down here, somehow. It's a mixed bag: French architects, German engineers, Australian technicians, British nurses, Irish vets, New Zealand firefighters, Argentinean doctors, Canadian physiotherapists. Expat upon expat in T-shirts and shorts. Even the dress code gives me shudders. We would be so deported if our attendance here gets out. Although, Charlotte's already getting deported. I slink down the beach.

"Girls!" Ringo smooches. He clings to Charlotte overly long.

Charlotte's showing signs of emotional wear-and-tear. Ringo hands us vodka shots. Then tequila shots. Then Jaegermeister shots. Then Jack Daniels with Red Bull. I spot Nick and a few other paid friends make their way over the sand dunes.

"Nick'll tell the nannies I was here!"

"No, he won't," Ringo soothes.

"How do you know?"

"Because he doesn't want it getting back to his VIP that he's here either."

Nick barely nods at me. I barely nod back. It's a

Mexican standoff. Charlotte drags me into the fray to dance. I am a twirling, stumbling invertebrate jellyfish. Where's my flagpole, where's my podium? If I had either I wouldn't be up on it, that's for sure.

People dance, everyone drinks, couples disappear behind dunes. At three in the morning, Charlotte and I decide to leave but by then a French architect, Manu, is attached at the hip to Charlotte and won't understand plain English to bugger off. Charlotte finally relents to give him a ride home and that's how we crash her beautiful, off-the-container-ship pristine Mercedes.

Manu yabbers in the back seat. None of us wears seatbelts. Our feet are barren and sand is everywhere.

The road suddenly transforms from a highway to a construction site, and Charlotte doesn't register the road works in time and we hit a pylon, fly through the air and I think, I've done this before, and relax into it as we embed the Mercedes on a steel block one foot wide by fifteen long that was supposed to hold up an off-ramp, but is now part of the engine block. Air bags explode in our faces. My body slides underneath the massive pillow. It smells like a car wreck. Manu has no airbag and facebutts my headrest, cutting his face open. My big toenail rips off. Charlotte's torso smashes into the steering wheel—she cannot speak.

I relaxed because I have survived a car wreck before. With dear Jacqui. What happened was she was seventeen and I was fifteen, it was raining and I let her drive. Back then you could get your driver's license at the age of fifteen and let me tell you I jumped for that independence and passed my written and practical tests first pop. Jac had more trouble with the practical. It didn't help that Dad's Vauxhall Viva passenger seat was broken and the driving test practitioner fell backwards into the back seat while Jac fluffed her hill start. Thus Jac was still on a learner's permit, and legally she could only drive with an older co-driver than me. She didn't listen as I said, "Slow down, Jac, slow down…" taking the bend too fast in the greasy rain, she overcorrected and *bam!!! smack!!!* we skidded 180° and smashed through a metal barrier, ripping my door off, and rolled three times like a crocodile in a death spin down an embankment. We stopped upside down in a totaled car with Michael Jackson's 'Billie Jean' blaring through the AIWA stereo.

We crawled from the steaming, hissing wreck, and hitchhiked home where I lied that I was the driver, not Jacqui, because it was our cousin's car and we didn't want to mess up his insurance.

The seatbelts saved our lives. No airbags back in 1987.

We crawl from the steaming, hissing wreck and I call Ringo who rescues us and deposits moaning Manu to his executive apartment for big babies. His French bleating really, really, really gets on my nerves. I've never been so angry at someone. Why didn't he just zip it and let Charlotte concentrate on the road rather than distract her with declarations of love?

There is something so self-indulgent about Manu's irrational 'love' and its consequences that puts me off the French for a long, long time.

Meanwhile, Charlotte still cannot speak. But we don't go to the Medical Center to see if we are concussed. That would take too much explaining.

The next morning, I see a local doctor who gamely drills a hole in my other big toenail in case that drains the blood and saves it from coming off. (It doesn't.) I hobble.

Ringo tells us that Manu, the big French loser, went to the Medical Center and needed stitches. I am petrified he gossiped about who else was in the car. That would get me fired.

I shuffle into the Sports Complex. My feet are swollen and blue.

Nick, green over his coffee, mumbles that Andre Agassi and Brooke Shields are coming over this afternoon so I need to organize snacks down at the Tennis Court.

I nod. It hurts my head to nod.

"Hey, your friend, what's her name?"

"Charlotte."

"Does she have a boyfriend?"

"Her contract wasn't renewed. She leaves tomorrow."

"Ah."

I tell the waitresses that I wore the wrong shoes and gave myself blisters.

Brooke barely lets go of Andre's hand to let him serve

balls to our sporty VIP, who's hyped up and charges the net. The pair look terrified they'll be cannibalized any second. I get some grit in my eyes and stand there, red eyed, tears winding their way down my cheeks, the blinkety-blink girl who can't seem to *walk*.

The toughest nanny rings (the one who *really* manages House Y), "Where are you now?"

"You just saw me cross the courtyard."

"Huh. What happen your feet?"

"I wore the wrong shoe."

"Huh. Mommy VIP say all Laundry Go Home Thailand. They burn her dress." Click.

Another female VIP letting her fury rip on the poor laundry team. I hobble down to investigate. Sawat, the cheerful, tiny woman in charge of the crew sits on the white tiles in tears. Thai music screams over the juddering, frothing, steaming, foaming machines. Tek kindly turns down the transistor so I can hear myself think. But I can't think.

"What happen, Sawat?"

"Mommy's maid bring so many sarong. We wash all thing and iron, but maid come and say they must take now. They say they finish iron sarong in the house. Then Nanny phone and say Mommy sarong all burn. But we not iron, the maid iron."

Unfortunately the maids have better 'access' to those in power and all seven laundry staff return to Bangkok within two days, just like Charlotte. Visa revoked, identity card taken, Bank of Xamnesia account closed, one month's pay bestowed.

There is no solidarity among nationalities working here. The Thai maids don't speak up for the laundry staff, just as Justine doesn't put in a word for Charlotte. It's all so arbitrary that it makes me yank out a load more eyelashes and make more wishes. *Something has to change! I want to stop feeling so powerless.* Unfortunately, I soon get my wish. After a holiday home.

18
―――
MEN 3

I am awarded annual leave. An economy class ticket has never been so beautiful.

House Y is 12,000 miles away from my old haunts but it's not far enough. How many times have I imagined myself home in Auckland and what I'd do there? Skip down Ponsonby Road to go for a coffee with real milk and real coffee and real newspapers and magazines about the real world, buying clothes designed for real females not Asian midgets, clothes that look gorgeous on me, hail friends who I bump into on sidewalks with no storm drains and no dead rats in them the size of kittens, wearing a coat it's so blissfully *chilly*?

Once home, I'm awash with a yellow-bellied paranoia of being scrutinized. I'm tongue-tied, vague and answer in riddles. I put my phone on every café table as if it's a live hand grenade and have stupid freak outs when my battery dies. Questions make my stomach heave and slither like a sack of black eels. My voice is horribly bright and breezy. Not my real voice.

Everyone believes I went to a Middle Eastern oasis of easy-living and glamour when really I'm a sleep-deprived, water-retaining freak with the communication skills of Swiss chess and the wardrobe of a manic depressive. I need my hair done by someone with a little more experience than Idora on vodka and Red Bull, armed with a box of 'Naturally Fair,' yet I miss Idora and Charlotte like they are the only two people who 'get it' in the entire world. Even when I get my hair done at the nicest salon in Auckland, it doesn't have that buzz that Idora's giggling butchering had. That, 'Hell, girl, we are living this, ha ha, so funny, screwed-up Xamnesia gig but we are not changing one iota, right?'

I go into manic overdrive. I rewrite that in my mind as doing what everyone wants of me. But the mania is all mine. I get four hours' sleep a night between a daft schedule of seeing a zillion friends and family, racking up bills in cafes, restaurants, bars, and clothing boutiques. I pick up every tab. I leave embarrassingly large tips for waitresses and barmen.

I tirelessly explain that I don't work for 'the Sheikh who owns half the world' but nobody listens to a word I say. I am that girl who was whisked out of Auckland overnight, to live a life of luxury and possibly do some sort of job as well. I am an alien revisiting my home planet only to find an impulse to nuke the place.

Nobody notices that I am a shell of my former self, if that self ever existed, since I've recently come to the conclusion that I've been a squirmy worthless nothing *since birth*.

And in turn, I can't understand the people who are supposed to be my best friends and family.

I am numb, even here, back home, where I thought I'd bounce back in a flash to normal Lizzie, or Liz, in the time it takes for jetlag to wear off. This really scares me but I squash that thought deep. Because if I don't bounce back here after a few days… then I might as well return to Xamnesia. My novel's half done. They just gave me another year's contract. I'd be a fool not to go back.

I meet up with the guy I fancied, Solomon, for coffee —he and I faxed a lot when I left for Xamnesia and had a simmering fascination for each other during my bar-hopping months. We meet in Vulcan Lane at the trendiest little café in that cobblestoned bastion of Auckland chic. I order a flat white. He leans across the mosaic-topped round table and takes my cold hands in his warm ones. His muscles ripple beneath his thin white shirt. He's a cyclist and a triathlete—is that even a word?—he always kept the drinking under control when we talked late at night at Dragon Bar or Crowbar. When we talked and flirted *a lot*.

"I have a confession," Solomon starts.

"Go ahead," I smile.

He tells me that I was part of an 'experiment' he was conducting with five women. My smile drops.

At first, the experiment was to flirt with all five women. Then, when I announced I was leaving for

Xamnesia things took a turn: he decided to tell all of us he loved us to see what would happen.

I edge back in my seat. I remember it well, how he professed that he loved me the night before I left Auckland. I didn't take it super seriously. But this confession of his hurts. His faxes kept me going for months—thinking that no matter how weird and confidence-crushing Xamnesia got, I had one normal guy back home who genuinely cared for me, and with whom I hadn't disgraced myself by sinking to a one-night stand or 'Sunday night' arrangement with. One bright untarnished star in my mottled, midnight-blue love life.

"So, what happened?" I ask brightly.

"After telling you all I loved you, I kept up relationships with you all—although you, my dear, was via fax. Things progressed, it got a little complicated," he sits back in his chair with a look of glee. "Then I decided to tell you all, face to face, about the experiment. One had left her husband for me; she returned to her marriage. One became a heroin addict. One reacted with a great deal of anger. Another had dropped out of law school to be with me... and we're still together. You were kind of the 'control' because you were so far away so it's taken all this time to be able to tell you, face to face..."

The rest of our coffee I can see him studying me, gauging my reaction. Will I take up heroin over him?

I cut the coffee short. Pay the bill. Leave a big tip. I laugh it off and give him a brief hug good-bye, but Solomon's little 'experiment' rattles me in all those ways I can't verbalize and choose to push out of my mind rather than examine up close and sift through. I internalize it immediately as me not being worthy of his sincere feelings. Am I still so clueless about men? I thought he saw me as a real, live person. But no, I am one fifth of an experiment.

I go to This is Not a Love Shop to look for second-hand treasures, but a Closed-Down sign dangles in the window, which makes me cry right there on Dominion Road like a total idiot.

My former roommates are taken aback by the smoking, but they suppose that in the international milieu of Xamnesia, this too is normal.

I meet an investor guy, Gary. Gary's some sort of acquaintance of Scottie's, has fished trout with him at Lake Taupo, he apparently knows my former bosses at Toto's, he buys champagne at SPQR to sit and drink, where he spiels that if I invest my savings with him, he can guarantee 20 percent compound interest because he's a stock market genius. He adds that he's been bankrupt before so there's *no way* he'll lose my money and cheerily namedrops other people known to me and how much they've all invested. I promise to transfer my US$61,000 in savings as soon as I'm back home in Xamnesia.

I spend two days with Charlotte in Bali on the way back.

"You're sure you want to go back, Lizziegirl?"

"What else should I do? I'm scared I'll blow everything I've saved and end up with nothing."

"What about your writing?"

"There's time later, when I'm inevitably fired, right?"

Charlotte is hanging out in Bali on a normal backpacker's budget as if she has nothing sitting in the bank. She's still savvy. I see how she's returned to the sassy, assured Charlotte I met in Xamnesia. I look at her and imagine that I'll be back to my old self once the Xamnesian conditioning wears off, like a sunburn that has to peel. I decide that Auckland made me act like such a freak. When I do leave Xamnesia, I just need to ensure I don't return *there* because it's such a goldfish bowl.

Even strong gorgeous Charlotte has a moment of regret when I hug her good-bye at Denpasar Airport.

"I should've behaved in the desert," she sighs. "I might not be living in this limbo if I'd sat on my hands like a good girl."

19

MEN 4

I am moved from Seven Story White Building to Happiness Apartments—into a two-bedroom apartment on Justine's floor. In the lobby, a security guard logs in everyone's comings and goings. Being at Happiness isn't the sun-moon-and-stars validation I imagined it would be. I become a solitary thing, who hides under my floral duvet to watch pirated movies and snarf instant noodles.

    I decorate my lounge with candles and an enormous hunk of driftwood with incense poking like armadillo's quills from all available crevices. I get a black cat I name Malteaser who only seems to eat his dry food when I join him on the floor and stroke his head. It reminds me of how Mom patted sick Jac's head across the Canadian prairies.

    Justine rings me one Thursday afternoon and grants

me my wish. Something changes. Why oh why did I wish for that?

"The key VIP would like to see you," she announces. "Eight o'clock, tonight." My mind floods with panic.

Captain's words jump into my head: 'huge honor.' It's a huge honor for the waitresses to be 'seen' by our key VIP. I remember how his eyes filled with empathy when I was so tongue-tied meeting him beside his toilet for thirty seconds.

I only see our eminent boss at a distance. I'm so busy avoiding crucifixion by nannies at House Y that I never give him much thought. I don't realize that when Justine says she'll put in a good word for me to gain a better position that she means *this*.

"Oh my God, I don't want to. Tell him no."

"He's flying to London tomorrow, so it has to be tonight."

"But I don't *like* him."

"It's a VIP request."

"Can't you go instead?"

"It's just how he is," Justine's getting tetchy.

"Look, I don't want this. Tell him I've got my period. Please."

"Oh, for Pete's sake," Justine hangs up. But she rings back.

"He doesn't mind. You don't have to do anything you don't want to do. But you have to go, Lizzie. Eight o'clock."

I know he rings her everyday to chat. She's confessed to her involvement with him. She calls it 'naughty mode.'

Says he's really good. But to bully her friend into private audiences with him? Maybe I'm easy to 'offer' to him because we are friends. She knows I don't dig him. It's horrible but I really feel I have no choice but to go.

I drive to a tiny satellite property tucked down a blink-and-miss-it turn between Houses X and Y. One security guard stands in a little guardhouse day and night. I park invisibly around the side and slink in the only door.

I'm not sure if I can talk about this but since I consider this to be outside of my employment contract and as it's my private life, not his, here goes.

It's one big room with two bathrooms off one end: one for the VIP, the other for 'Guest.' Everything else is King-Sized Bed and Swimming Pool. I won't go into the décor. Let's just say marble and silk are staples. My legs turn to jelly so I go into the Guest Toilet and grip the marble sink surround, staring at the lined-up toiletries in a pretense of being here to see them, not him.

In the kitchenette, waitresses left the standard 'Snacks' set out in countless corners every day, in case the key VIP drops by. Fresh cut fruit (no papaya, of course, as this nation of people believe papaya can render their men impotent), a small plate of biscuits, two bottles of mineral water at room temperature. If only I had a load of papaya to pelt him with, disabling his virility.

A wall screen glows blue ready for whatever the VIP wants to watch and I can take one guess about that.

There isn't even an innocent chair to sit on. Just that enormous bed with ivory silk sheets turned down.

Can I pretend I don't follow his drift? Play super dumb and quote Justine's 'I don't have to do anything I don't want to.' I hesitate, but turn off my phone at 7:59.

I hear his car roar into the driveway two minutes later and brace myself. The doors swing inwards and he bops down the stairs and grabs my hands, turning my palms upward in his.

"Hello, Lizzie. You have cold hands. Cold hands, warm heart."

I don't find him sexy. He's wiry and says weird things. I feel sick and jittery with this unwarranted male attention directed on me like a laser beam. And I know I'm unable to walk out of this or talk my way out of this. I'm back on the Barrier with that huge man throwing me between his legs and twirling me around—I am drifting away, 38,000 feet up into the sky where it's quiet and I am home—safe. I feel nothing but detachment.

He sits on the edge of his giant bed and strips off his clothes in a blink, so fast I don't even register if he wears underwear or not, and then he stands, body taunt (for his age, a good twenty years older than me), taking me by the hand toward his giant swimming pool. *I wear contact lenses, I hate swimming*, I want to say. Nothing comes out of my mouth.

"Do you swim?"

"Not really."

"It's very warm."

He steps into the water.

"I was telling the truth. I have my period," I cringe. Surely that should be the equivalent of papaya?

"That's alright," his voice echoes off the tomblike marble. "Come in."

He's halfway up the pool, leaving me to undress without scrutiny. This is not a level playing field.

I slip off my clothes, feeling ungainly, and sink into the water. Maybe I can drown myself. But I know I won't. I will grit my teeth and get through this.

The water is 79°F, hot. He's reached the other end.

"Now you swim to this end and I go to your end, yes?"

So he makes me swim laps for half an hour.

No wonder we were encouraged to go to the gym. I am out of shape. I struggle along with breaststroke and side crawl, keeping my face (contact lenses) out of the water. He does free style and I don't look to see what else. He's fast. I'm like an inept dog needing a lifebuoy. I lose count of the laps, but I'm at the shallow end when he asks if I want a breather. I need a new set of lungs. I pant, which is not at all what I want him to hear.

"You don't swim much?" he chuckles. I want to punch him in the groin.

I shake my head. *No time, Sir, between my pathetic existence at the worst property in this fucked-up country of yours, Sir... and my extra-curricular activities of illegal partying and occasional bad sex with one of your son's paid friends, a commitmentphobe... you know the type.* But I'm incapable of speech. I seriously hate this swimming. At this stage, I will do whatever's required just to get out of this stifling water. Why is he doing this?

He plays with the remote controls, placed conveniently at his end and porn splatters across the giant wall screen. Oh, shit. He's serious.

"Look there... she's coming, you see?"

The sight of a blonde in orgasm, or faking it, lights up his entire face.

She's pretending. She's regretting not paying her union dues now. She hates herself, Sir, my silent self blathers. In reality, I wince. I wasn't ever a big fan of porn. It always looks so badly filmed.

The bleached blonde arches in real or faked ecstasy. Close-up of a thick penis penetrating her fills the screen and he's beside me now, his arm grips me around my waist, and his tongue weasels into my mouth.

"Her pussy likes it, don't you think?"

His fingers feel the edges of me and the on-screen blonde makes a hell of a racket, this time being pumped hard from behind.

"Come."

He darts up the pool stairs, nimble as a goat, trailing me by the hand. Water runs off my body and he surveys me with delight in his black eyes.

"I love bottoms like yours."

I almost choke. It's a booty, with cheeky cellulite. It's an hourglass ass, not a model's butt. He hones right in on the part of my body I hate.

He presses a vibrator hard against my pubic bone and within a minute I orgasm. Not like her on the screen, whose guttural moaning now sounds like a farmyard animal dying, but in a silent, shaky way, and he deftly lowers me onto his huge bed, flicks on a condom and goes for it until he groans a little and lays on my chest. He kisses me once more. Then gets out the vibrator again.

"That was very nice for me," he says in a robotic voice. He gestures over my torso and adds, "Keep it for me."

I non-answer with a vague twist of my lips.

I go to the Guest Toilet, aware that I've streaked up the pristine silk sheets with my embarrassing female functions. Silk sheets that the laundry guys at House X will half kill themselves to get clean.

If I had self-esteem issues before, they just upped to loathing myself. How could I let that happen? I have nobody to blame but myself. I will never speak of this. Ever.

I sneak back into my clothes that lie poolside. Thankfully, the porn's off, so I don't have to see further scenes of shame spread three yards wide. He's in his VIP toilet, perhaps deciding he no longer wants a certain toiletry item. I figure he'll leave straightaway, since he's gotten what he was after.

But he emerges, wrapped in a green silk dressing gown and proceeds to make us both a Gregg's Red Ribbon Roast in the kitchenette.

"Do you take milk? Sugar?"

"Uh, yes, one sugar and milk. Thank you."

He opens the real milk for me. Not even UHT fake milk. The real, airflown stuff. I perch on the bed as there's nowhere else to sit, and sip soundlessly.

Here's my big chance to plead Charlotte's case to get

her her job back, or bitch about the evil nannies at House Y, or ask why was I kicked out of House X? To get political. But I don't want to talk to him. I don't want to owe him anything. I don't want to share.

"How's House Y?"

"Fine, Sir."

"Good, good." He polishes off his coffee and dresses in another sleight of hand. "I'll see you, Lizzie," he beams, mounting the stairs to the door. Seconds later I hear his car fire up and blast off.

I take in the scene of my moral disintegration—messed-up red-streaked bed, water puddles, blue screen ready again, empty china teacups, torn corner of a condom wrapper, and then walk out to return to House Y and stand at the back wall of the Sports Complex, happily invisible once again.

This is already erased from memory.

20
SILENCE 3

Mom and Dad are coming to Xamnesia to visit.

I have five minutes before leaving for the airport to pick them up. I'm nervous and light a cigarette off the gas stovetop, but lean over too close and singe off half an eyebrow. Ouch. Great. The smell of burnt human hair will be their welcome.

Mom *cannot* know I'm a smoker. They weren't in New Zealand when I recently visited and have no idea of my latest habit. Mom would be angry and worry. Worrying Mom may result in death—hers or mine I can never tell.

The pick-up at the airport goes fast, no customs' disembowelment of their solitary suitcase.

Dad's nose twitches when he walks into the apartment and Mom frowns. Maybe I can claim I have a voodoo dolly out back I must perform incendiary rituals on to perpetuate this cushy gig in Xamnesia.

They are shorter than I remember and Dad cracks jokes about Mom cracking jokes about moving here. It's strange to see them here: Mom with her Rapunzel-length hair snuggled into a high bun, her pastel clothes, her kid leather moccasins. Not a wrinkle, even at sixty-seven. I wonder what face cream she uses.

Dad's mad-scientist curls are only graying at the sides, even at the age of seventy-five to my twenty-five. He wears the same brown leather belt made in one of us kids' leatherwork class from high school. Did I make that for him? Who can remember.

I am flighty. I talk non-stop. I interrupt their stories. I interrupt, but say nothing, I ask them questions but they're not big questions: Can we talk about what the hell I'm doing with my life? Does anyone wonder if I'm okay? Nah, it's miniscule questions: Do you want another Baileys? Did you have any dreams last night? Isn't it cool here in Xamnesia? You wanna go for a drive? I'll show you the waterfall. Let me show you the Playground. What do you fancy for dinner?

I make them climb the lookout in the midday heat to see a waterfall. Mom says she expected monkeys. I tell her wrong subcontinent. We go to the free Playground and watch the musical fountain and Mom says it's the grandest thing she's seen, while Dad says there was a similar water fountain in Rotorua (a town of 30,000 people where they lived in 1972—I kind of doubt it would be a comparable spectacle). Mom reprimands Dad. I take us to dinner to every possible restaurant: the Mexican place, the food fair in the mall, the Chinese with the 'special tea' beer in teapot phenomenon. They meet my friends: Justine, Ringo, the English security guard Elaine.

I would love for them to see something wrong and order me to leave with them—be taken 'home'—to be folded up into their suitcase and smuggled over the border.

I have a video camera, a SONY, the latest, with a color viewfinder; it was a Christmas present from my grumpy VIP of House Y. I film them. Mom's uncomfortable; Dad's never sure when the camera's rolling, how much the mike will pick up, so he recounts his impressions in loud, painstaking detail. He goes into great specifics of how he had a sore tooth and so I took him to Medical Center.

"A facility owned by the SHEIKHS," he hollers. The dentist checked his blood pressure, checked his mouth for cancer, then pulled the tooth, painlessly, but it broke up due to the rot and the shards had to be dug out.

"It's all completely pain free today though…" he yells chirpily. "Of course, the NEXT-DOOR TOOTH has to be filled, which I suspect will have to occur back in Canada… as there was decay BETWEEN the two teeth in question."

"The whole thing cost, how much, Vic?"

"25 *drachmas*. That's XAMNESIAN money. That's roughly $10 Canadian."

"All that, for ten dollars," Mom marvels.

The jokes about moving here don't end. They could just squat in my spare bedroom, pat the cat while I'm at work so the poor thing eats more. The Sheikh, or whoever I work for would never notice. Mom doesn't even find it hot.

"Sure, it's a little muggy, but it's just like Canada… everyone has air-conditioning there."

Here's me thinking I'm living in an extreme situation, and yet to them this place is no different to Canadian sitting rooms, or small-town New Zealand from the seventies. Phew.

I try to make them understand that normally I'm working extremely long hours with no days off. That this is blind luck because my VIP and his mother are overseas right now. But I'm not sure they hear me.

Mom makes a raft of jokes about how much she approves of this Muslim culture. "A young lady should always be chaperoned (preferably by her mother)." There's that no sex before marriage (or possibly within marriage) thing again. Maybe Mom *does* want a job here, as Moral Crusader.

"Now, Liz, do you know what to do with money?"

This is the fourth day. Mom's an insomniac, up reading her Patricia Cornwell murders until late then sleeping until midday. Dad's up at 7:00 a.m. everyday, offering porridge (which I have never eaten in my life, he's confusing me with other children but the offers never let up). Mom corners me in the kitchen, a nervous twinkle in her eye, clutching her solar pocket calculator that she carries everywhere.

"Now, if you have, say… US$60,000 saved, you just put it in a high-interest rate savings account and then you'll get 10 percent interest—and you live off *that*. That way you'll never touch the principle."

"Mom. Don't worry about me."

As soon as she offers guidance I back away. She never asks me how much money I've made. She pretends she doesn't want to know anything, yet clearly she's thinking about it a lot. And where does she think I can live on US$6,000 per year? Bulgaria? Mexico? She must think I have way more than that. *Shit. I don't.*

Plus I've invested my sixty thousand with Mr. 20-Percent-Compound-Interest. With his assurances, spreadsheets, stock names, and case studies.

Mom grew up in the Depression, I remind myself. She's from a world of meatloaf as a special occasion, and the One-Dollar Shop, and not throwing dinner parties or going out, and one pot of face cream per year. They probably *do* live off about US$6,000 a year.

I flashback to that European trip where I made my US$1,500 last from May until November, give or take. *It's good advice*, something inside me says. *Go live in a village somewhere cheap and write. Listen to your mom. LIVE OFF the interest.* But there's something about Mom's ways that I want to reject and prove somehow that I am destined to make a bigger splash in the world. A bigger splash by listening to what some guy called Gary buying champagne at SPQR says. I'm after the easy money. The compound interest. The risky gamble. I think I know how to play poker.

I respect the One-Dollar Shop and love meatloaf, but there was a big sense of *playing safe* and *not-enough* that went along with Mom's code of conduct. I always wanted to have friends stay over (never could), or friends round to play (never allowed), and a mother who baked (didn't happen), and to live in a tidy house (nope, not that either). Mom *had seven of us*. She officially gave up on housework and birthday-cake-baking circa 1984 after which I baked the birthday cakes (it's true, Mr. Malik, I did adore the decorating side, I have gorgeous photos of my piped icing) and got out the Lysol spray and Hoover when the mess overwhelmed me.

But friends were still only rarely allowed over. My best friend from high school invited me over so often I called her dad, Mister Dad. I floated into other people's homes. I was allowed to sleep over at my boyfriend's parents' place—even though they were the same age as mine, they didn't care if pre-marital sex was going on downstairs. But the only time I sneaked him into our house I made him hide under the covers when Dad poked his head in to the room to say good morning.

It was all so fraught. I moved out so I could have friends over. I couldn't cope with Mom's rigid rules.

I find myself ticked off with Mom's worldview right now because I'm emotionally invested in Xamnesia. I'm working 100 hours per week. This *has* to be a good choice and I *have* to know what I'm doing because I'm in it for the second year and to admit otherwise means I'm lost and need help and have a boatload of issues.

I don't want to make do with one pot of face cream per year. I want—not La Prairie—but at least Clinique. Lots of Clinique. To slather Clinique. To throw the pot away not completely scraped out. To get away from this dragging sense that I won't be seeing any other money and I'll have to live off US$6,000 per year.

"Okay, Mom, thanks for that. Shall we drive over to the New Mosque? Foreigners are allowed inside on Tuesdays."

With one day of Mom and Dad's visit remaining, my phone rings at 4:30 a.m.

It's Mr. Malik, in London. The hollering is like being flailed. *"House Y is on fire. You go there and find out which motherfucker do this and you set that MOTHERFUCKER on fire."*

I scrawl a shaky note for my parents and am on-site within fifteen minutes. The firemen are all grisly Kiwis, called Bob, Rob or Wayne. They've extinguished the flames but the main house is not yet cleared to enter. The Chief explains that the fire started on the top floor—in one of the adopted daughters' bedroom. Maybe from a frilly lamp. White and black smoke curl out the front door. Captain from X House is here, grilling our In-Charge Security Guard here, who smiles guilelessly looking almost proud to be hosting such an exciting event.

The thing about House Y was that the security guards were lazy and often drunk on Mekong whisky, which was paint-strippingly strong shit. How many times had I seen red flashes on the fire alarm panel ignored? Hundreds.

And our In-Charge was more interested in kick-backs and corrupt going's-on than running an effective team.

Yes. Lizzie finds herself among criminals, again.

"How could a child's lamp cause a fire—it wouldn't even have been turned on with the family traveling?"

No answer.

The firemen clear the building for entry. The stink of burned silk and wool chokes and burns my eyes. The ground floor is mainly smoke and water damaged. I can't describe the luxurious elements of the mansion's interior, but let's just say silk is not flame-retardant.

Captain is on the phone to the VIP's butlers. His face puckers in fury. My phone rings.

"*What have those motherfuckers done with the VIP's boxes?*" Mr. Malik roars.

Oh. It's arson to nick valuables. If there is one thing I can say about the interior of House Y, it's that expensive stuff sat piled high in boxes in every direction. Boxes were never put away because that would involve asking the VIP where they wanted to put something. Nobody close to these people asked that sort of question.

"*Those motherfuckers think they can start a fire and steal VIP thing, I fly back and fuck them all!*" Malik bellows.

In-Charge swears that nothing was removed.

Captain gets real precise; his eyes a knife's slit, describing how high the piles of boxes should be in the bedroom and landing according to the butlers, and how low they are now. In-Charge suggests the Kiwi firemen stole the boxes.

He really is that shameless.

Mr. Malik fires all the security guards who were on

shift that day and night. The nicest of the Switchboard operators, Chol, takes over.

Many many 'VIP Thing' too private to be listed are never recovered. I do feel a small sense of vindication because I'd been telling anyone who'd listen that House Y's security guards were the most corrupt I'd heard of in this country. They blew it for themselves. For high-end watches and moon memorabilia. Where were they going to sell that stuff?

Mom and Dad's final twenty-four hours in Xamnesia are spent alone. I see them only to rush them to the airport. After assuring them there is no public transport here, Dad found a bus that took them downtown, where they toodled happily, seeing more sights in one day than I have in a year and three months here. I hug them goodbye at the departure lounge.

Mom's forehead wrinkles, "You smell of smoke."

I tell them I love them and they wave cheerily.

"Take care," is what Mom says.

I watch my video footage of Mom and Dad at the waterfall and hanging out in my kitchen. When my phone rang at one stage, I passed the camera to Mom, who was supposed to continue capturing Dad's monologue about the wonders of the dentist.

She hushed Dad and panned around to me, sitting on the kitchen counter, talking low to Nick who rang from London about installing an additional TV screen in the Sports Complex. I'm all bright-voiced, cheery efficiency, asking clarifying questions, ringing off with polite servile gratitude. Sneaky Mom was trying to hear something of what my job really entails. She never asked a thing point blank. (But what would I have said? Precisely nothing in reply.)

It's quite chilling to see Xamnesia in action when I look at myself on film. There's such a desperate edge to my voice—'I'm being good! I'm here to help!'—then when I return to the kitchen table I brush off Mom's, "Everything alright?" with total indifference. It is the saddest thing I've seen in a long time.

I ring Idora, at work in London. She does a great job of bolstering long distance. But I tell myself if something nice doesn't happen pronto, I'm out of here.

21

MOVEMENT 4

Something nice happens. My sullen VIP needs some help sticking to his new diet and I become his official calorie counter. I can't go into detail of all the meals I concoct to keep him happy, but the role actually thrills me. I am legitimate. I am in his team. I now travel with him to supervise his meals. I'm no longer wallpaper in the Sports Complex. He even speaks to me.

Usually it's: "What's the yellow stuff, Lizzie?"

"Parsnip mash, Sir."

"It's awful."

"Yes, Sir, sorry."

But, still. Take that, mean nannies. Lizzie is useful and competent.

My VIP is young. As young as me. Twenty-five and flying his own private plane. (Literally. First time I saw him disappear into the cockpit I figured he was inspecting the pilot's work, but he had a pilot's license.) He never asks to 'see' me and those two hours spent with his father are long gone from my memory. Months fly by.

And Daisy is still there as a role model of how to handle tricky, tricky Xamnesia.

First time on the private plane, she pats the seat next to her. I am a member of her club now; the paid friends greet me like a long-lost sister—which never happens in the Sports Complex, Daisy wants me to sit beside her.

"So you're doing his food now," she says with her odd smile.

"Yeah. So what do you do on the trips?"

"Help out."

With what, I wonder? "You have to carry his phone when he's traveling?"

That's all I glean Daisy actually does.

"There's a lot more to it than that."

The sports friends high-five Daisy like she's their personal cheerleader. Which I guess is the nicest job description I can think of for her.

I settle into the huge seat and figure maybe it'll be nice having someone like me to hang out with. Again, I'm on the lookout for my new pack, this time a traveling pack.

Every trip, some high-up member of staff corners me in the corridor, whips out a sheet of paper and a tiny Mont Blanc pen, crosses my name off a list and presses an Envelope into my hands.

"As thanks for traveling," the person will wink.

"Oh! You're very welcome."

I slip the Envelope into my waistband and find a staff toilet to lock myself into.

It's generally US$15,000. In massive, crimson ten-thousand *drachma* bills.

Tired tears always spring to my eyes. These bills are so massive and beautiful and clean. Like nothing bad could ever result from them. They are so new they give me paper cuts.

Then I wonder how much does Daisy get? For virtually nothing. It can't be nothing, can it? Can you really be part of the entourage and do zip? There's no such thing as a free lunch, but is there here? Then again, what do I know? Maybe her job is to watch lame movies and crack jokes.

Daisy comes over to my hotel room and orders pizza, which she gobbles most of. My phone rings so I retreat to the corridor outside and when I return she's in the toilet and I hear, "Out!! Get out, you bitch!!" and then horrendous vomiting.

Daisy emerges, eyes a little watery, but no other sign.

"Are you okay?"

She looks at me like I have two heads. "Of course."

I don't feel jealous of that.

Christmas morning, 1997, I'm let off the diet carousel to shop. This is completely the opposite of my Christmas morning two years ago, when we realized we'd been burgled. But actually, it's not that different. The effects of counting calories and concocting meals see me full of anxiety and panic attacks.

I run like a skinned cat around the beautiful, pristine department store of the major city I'm in, shopping mindlessly: Ralph Lauren, Giorgio Armani, Calvin Klein. More pantsuits. More shoes. Plain Jane tops and boring tailored trousers. I can't see if anything looks good on me or not, I swallow and hand over cash.

Things do look good on me. Because while Daisy's bulimic, I'm practically anorexic. I eat one meal per day: lunch. Nothing for breakfast. Alcohol for dinner. Cigarettes peppered throughout the day. I've dropped to 105 pounds for a height of five foot five.

I used to love those Saturday afternoons of trawling shops with my friends, finding sassy-girl, nightclub-podium dancing items or saving for months to go and formally purchase one sale-discounted item from Zambezi or World. I can't shop alone. I can't do anything alone. What am I if I can't walk through a department store without *having a panic attack*?

I grab gifts for my family that I post from the hotel I'm in for the week. I buy gallons of perfume to mask cooking smells and the scent of cigarettes. I try to buy myself a bra but I don't have the heart for it.

US$5,000 dollars goes in two hours. More than my college loans I was so freaked about when I arrived in Xamnesia. Triple what I lived off in Europe for half of a year. Gone in two hours.

22

MISCHIEF 3

For the end of Ramadan celebrations, I get a diamond Jaegar Le Coultre Reverso with diamonds. And US$15,000. I keep counting calories.

"We have a problem with the staff," Mr. Malik barks down the phone. Somebody's brought it to somebody's attention that Thailand's equivalent of *Hello!* or *The Inquirer* ran a six-page scoop about 'Life inside Xamnesia': with photos of Thai maids and waitresses posing on the furniture, playing Lady of the Manor. We have to search the staff housing to see what other photos have been taken.

I assume the repercussions will be a Malik-style telling off, which is nothing to be sniffed at, not realizing at first that of course, anyone in breach of the rules of conduct will be sent packing. Staff is not informed. It's a raid.

At dawn, we comb through the female staff's apartments.

It's the most disgusting 'job' I've ever done. Worse than cleaning an old folks' home all summer when I was fourteen. Way worse than my first waitressing job at La Ferrari Pizzeria where the owner's hand slid around my waist anytime he squeezed by. This tops everything.

This is no human rights.

And the effort of checking their belongings exhausts us. Rifling through photo albums. Peering at film negatives. There are ninety four-bed apartments to invade and wade through. I'm less of a human than how I woke up.

What we uncover is that these women hoard. Boy, do they hoard. They have dried mango in their underwear drawers. Apples under their pillows. Containers of cooked rice in their bedside cupboards.

Then, some have not been behaving. They have gold cutlery stashed under mattresses. Whisky in their closets. Entire albums of photos taken inside the palaces. Logoed towels and bedding, china and crystal, ashtrays with VIPs initials lasered onto them. Things they claim are gifts.

Far worse is the beautifully stacked clothes and neatly folded underwear. The carefully pressed blouses hanging ready for their next shift. The well-worn bowtie of their work uniform taking pride of place in a crowded drawer. So many are only hiding photos of their babies and young children back in Thailand, being raised by relatives, far away from their mommy. So many hide nothing but framed photos of the Thai King.

Another slew of horror stories emerges. Gambling

rings are uncovered. Blackmailing among staff is unearthed. Everyone involved is sent home. One waitress jumps out a second floor window because she's in such gambling debt, and is sent home on crutches. I lose a maid from the Sports Complex—now I know why Moo was always asleep in the corner by the bowling alley—she was up all night at the camps. Prostitution filled the gap between what she hoped to make and what she was making because she never got to travel. And I have no power against the nannies to rotate the maids so that they all get a chance to travel and make those extra Envelopes.

Every deportee is repentant and begs for a second chance, but it's 'no' every time.

It's Daisy's turn. She's made redundant, or quits, it's unclear. She rings me, "Lizzie, can you come over?" I go and help her pack. She has a container of furniture to send by sea. Many many Samsonites. She eats pizza, giving me bottles of red wine, contemplating how to pack her enormous black sheepskin.

"That must be, what, ten skins?" I say, picking off only the olives to nibble.

"What do you mean, *skins*?"

"Sheepskins. How do you think they make those rugs?"

"They're not skins," Daisy's voice rises in confusion. "They shear the sheep, dummy and stick it, with glue, to the back of a rug."

I peel back the rug and contemplate the stitched-together pelts of ten dead lambs. I'm very tempted to explain the typical life of a sheep to her, she'd probably give me the sheepskin if she understood it, but then, do I really want a ten-dead-sheepskin to lug around in my life?

"Oh, I see what you mean, Daisy."

"I don't know how you're still here," she shakes her head.

"Sure, Daisy." I try a joke, "So, back home, are you going to get a job where people know what you actually do?"

No reply. Even in the final hour that girl keeps mum. I have to hand it to her: she was more pro than the rest of us put together. She was *made for* Xamnesia thinking.

We finish the second bottle and the maids leave, bowing to Daisy as she passes out tips and grins thanks: "*Kop khun ka!*"

"It's April Fool's Day, call your dad and play a prank," Daisy says.

So I ring. Dad picks up and I launch into this crazy story, barely keeping a straight face while Daisy rolls on her leather couch turning purple with laughter.

"Dad! Great news… I'm moving into 'the Palace'…"

"Oh? Why's that, kiddo?"

"Well, I'm marrying one of the VIPs. He's only eighty! Sixty-five years older than me! Pretty cool, huh? Plays chess…"

"What's that? How old?"

"Yeah, I'm getting very own wing in the palace, I'll be his tenth wife, but the others are okay about it…"

"What? What other wives? Don't you think you want to talk to your mother about all this?"

"It's cool, Dad, oh, and guess what? I'm pregnant!"

Daisy's eyes meet mine and we rock with champagne-fuelled laughter while my poor seventy-eight-year-old father's voice rises in increasing panic and we hear a terrible choking down the line.

"Dad? DAD? Are you okay?"

"Abort!!! Abort!!!" he chokes. "Abort it now!"

He goes into such a choking fit—that I'm scared he's having a heart attack.

"DAD!!! Dad. It's April Fool's! I'm sorry, Dad," I backtrack, running out of Daisy's, downstairs to my car. "That was a lousy joke. I'm so sorry."

"I meant it, kiddo. If you get into that kind of trouble."

"No. Of course, I'm not in that kind of trouble."

What the hell is wrong with me?

Jacqui swings through Xamnesia on her way to a new life in Sydney, Australia. She met a wonderful sexy French man, Eric, when she was skiing in Mirabel with her (now) ex-boyfriend. She actually met two wonderful sexy French men and had her pick. Eric lives in Sydney and they've kept up their instant love for each other since New Year's Eve. She is moving there to see how it goes.

But we know Jac. It'll go beautifully. She is made for being the girlfriend. Beach-pretty Jacqui is back in force.

In May 15, 1998, after counting 480,000 calories and devising 960 meals, I meet Finn—who becomes my Xamnesia boyfriend.

I drive to Ringo's after work, after ducking home to A) bribe the security guard *not* to log my imminent departure and B) a quick change out of my boring suit into jeans and a long-sleeved top. Illegal alcohol-fuelled party or not, I still dressed with respect for the conservative, teetotaler Muslim country I live in.

I visualize a beautiful shot of Absolut Vodka as I roll down the quiet cul-de-sac where Ringo has his own house. ACDC thumps from inside. Smoke from a machine curls out the front door. These parties are always a hazy, gyrating, sweaty, plastic-cup spilling, anonymously-crushing, cigarettes held aloft, mass of bodies getting shitfaced. People end up in the pool or upstairs in a bedroom. Or, like tonight, both. I also find this situation terrifying these days. Will someone see me and report that I'm at this event when I'm supposed to be a well-behaved property manager? I'm every kind of phobic and wish I had a Zorro mask handy. Too late, I've reached the bar.

Ringo grins and lines up three shots, all for me.

"Bottom's up, girl," he says. "Baileys, Absolut Mandarin, and Jager. I call that the Holy Ringo Trinity." He boots a South African land surveyor off the nearest bar stool and I perch on it like it's a pedestal.

I've been on my pedestal, or dancing, and I've definitely drunk too much to be sober, when I see a guy get pushed into the swimming pool and come up spluttering, soaked, lamenting in a strong Californian accent, "My phone's toast, now, you jerks."

He walks up to the bar, streaming chlorinated water and stands beside me, sheepish, holding his soaked Ericsson T28i like a fallen bird, asking Ringo if he has a hairdryer to try and dry the guts of the phone, hearing that it's upstairs and we can help ourselves, and I ask the guy if he'd like some help and he looks at me and says, "Yes."

Five minutes later we're on a bed, door locked, clothes peeled off in a sodden mass (his), dropped to the floor like a snake's skin (mine), hands running all over each other, mouths everywhere and then going for it like newlyweds. And I come back to life from the numb state of sensory deprivation I'm in. I am falling in love. This guy is tender, beautiful, okay, he's drunk like I am, but in this moment we are one beautiful thing together. I collapse on top of his warm, beating chest. The bed stops creaking. Motley Crue is audible through the thick stucco walls. It's so dark I can barely see his eyes.

"Whoa, girl. That was pretty wild."

Darn it, I got his accent all wrong. He's Australian, not Californian.

"What's your name?" he kisses me, running his hands up my torso as if it's written on me in Braille.

"Um, I don't usually do things like this," I non-answer.

23

CRASH 2

I play it cool with Finn. For five minutes. But it has to be said I am a mess these days, and unable to play anything, cool or fever-hot. Beyond the anorexia issue, I'm also so addicted to Red Bull that I needed at least one can to be safe on the roads in the mornings and I chug through a pack and a half of Virginia Slims menthol or Marlboro Lights per day. I'm not even sure which cigarette brand I smoke. I don't hang out with Justine anymore. Thank goodness I have a cleaner who feeds Malteaser or he'd have died of neglect by now.

So I ring Finn.

"Mystery Girl!" His Australian accent is ridiculous. I imagine he's a surfer. "I'm glad you called, angel."

That gets me, right there, his 'angel.'

But I don't jump in with more conversation, I'm much better at making other people do the talking.

"Are you still there?" Finn waffles, the dead air leaving him nervous.

"Uh-huh."

"So, do you wanna come round—hang out?" He sounds like he's biting his lip. I do have fond memories of those lips. As long as he keeps his mouth shut, then seeing Finn can't get me into hot water, can it?

Sure, Finn is probably an immature commitment-phobe with a drinking problem (modus operandi for expat guys here) but I enjoyed myself there on Ringo's spare bed. I actually forgot everything that's dragging me down (like how many calories an apple is). And when he was all sodden and concerned about fixing his phone, Finn looked as vulnerable as I feel. We may be soul mates.

"How do I find your place?" I say.

"You know where all the Medical Center nurses live? I'm after that."

"No."

"Down after the Irish vet's place."

"Sorry."

"The German car mechanics' street?"

"Not ringing any bells."

"You don't get out much, do you?"

This is true; I only know the way to House Y. "Can you meet me at the Thai Café and I'll follow you?"

"Sure."

I wait outside the Thai Café at midnight. Excited, although my eyes look hollow, my skin is deathly pale. I smoke, watching for Finn. A white Kijang pulls up, the heavy beat of Extreme breaking the stillness. We aren't going to be soul mates if this guy's a big fan of Australian metal. But then he rolls down his window and grins, and he's more than cute—he's beautiful. Tall, dark hair, green eyes, tanned and muscular, the complete stereotype of a sexy boyfriend.

"Follow me, angel."

Finn leads me down a road I don't know, pulling up to a rundown bungalow at the very end of the street. His house is blessedly hidden by palm trees. He's already opening my door. His hands are cool. As he leads me across the threshold, the removal of clothing commences.

My hands shake as I barrel down the staff driveway of House Y through the thin slice of hazy dusk.

I drive head-on into a white van.

The staff van.

My airbag explodes, suffocating me with its pillowy vastness. A smell of chemicals and broken car and oil fills the air. Oil. Ha, ha, that's what's propping up Xamnesia. I crawl out of my beloved car, staring at the steaming, accordioned front bonnet of my BMW in disbelief as Thai cooks and maids crowd around to hug me.

I feel their arms around me and snap to. What was I doing? Yes, driving like crazy back to House Y from the sports field because the waitress forgot our VIP's strawberry yoghurt for his snack.

I shrug off the warm hug.

"I'm fine, I'm fine. I just need another car."

I limp inside House Y.

Chol, our In-Charge has heard of my crash via walkie-talkie.

"Miss Lizzie," he looks me in the eye. "I request another car. It arrive in five minutes."

Nobody says, "Hey, have you lost the plot from feeding a certain VIP? Do you need to take a minute?"

I can hear Charlotte though. She's now living in Tokyo with an American photojournalist for TIME and I can hear her voice as if she's beside me, "Lizziegirl, screw the calorie count. Make up the totals. You think they'd notice?"

Idora, on the phone from London really does say, "Girl, what's with the car crash? You've got to take better care of you." Idora works fourteen-hour days with a permanent smile on her face, loving every minute of it. Why am I letting this get to me?

The lemon and poppy seed cookies are a problem, too. My initial calculation of them as fifteen calories crumbles when I realize my bakers started using real butter instead of the zero-calorie Becel out of fear of offending our VIP. Each heart-shaped cookie is more like fifty calories and our VIP imbibes so many per week he's probably hallucinating from the poppy seeds (they are a distant cousin to opium, after all).

I'm not sure I can keep juggling the calorie counting plus courting Finn's interest.

Finn is a tiny bit like a few other guys I've tried to date. I think I'm dating them. They think we're just screwing around in a happy non-committal way. When will I learn this one?

Finn's bungalow door's open. He's ironing his shirts. "Hey, angel. Wanna drink?"

"Sure, in a minute," I light a cigarette.

"Everything alright?"

"Yeah. And you?"

He looks at me, then his eyes dart away. I realize he hasn't even kissed me. I feel a chilly sense of premonition. God, I'm stupid. I keep walking into this exact scene. He shoots vapor, left and right. The comforting smell of laundry detergent muddled with steam and a tang of sweat rises around us.

"Go on, just tell me."

"Angel," he rests the hot iron, studying the board as if his lines are scribbled on his wrinkled shirts in invisible ink. "I'm an asshole, angel. A bloody shit. Not worth a fucking minute of your time. I slept with one of those Medical Center nurses at a party."

"Nice," I bite my lip. "Which one?"

He finishes the last panel of his shirt and gives it a nice hanger.

"Which what?" he pulls another crumpled shirt onto the board, eyes down.

"Which girl?"

"Aquilina."

Right. The ditzy, cute one from Essex with big tits. I wish I had a firearm.

"I should go."

He sighs. "Let's have a drink first, eh?"

I make my way to the kitchen to fix our usual Jack Daniels and Coke, a drink I don't even like, but I drink because that's what he drinks and I want to make it easy for him to be with me, it's part of my plaster of Paris I mold myself into for others. My vision blurs with my sense of failure and the fear that comes with it, that deflation that comes from letting your heart expand only to find everything trickled out because you're not worthy of another's love. It's hard to find my breath. Finn pulls me into one of his hugs, a fierce one, that tells me he wants to do things right, but isn't quite equipped. Or maybe it's to tell me he's got nothing to say.

"I'm going to go."

"I wish I'd met you about ten years ago before I turned into an asshole," he breathes into my hair.

"Or in another ten years when you stop being one."

I take my shriveled stomach and sadness straight over to Ringo's and after imbibing too many B52s, I have another car accident.

Except the car isn't moving. I get so drunk that I lurch outside to sit in my replacement BMW and pull myself together, but then feel sick and hear a roaring in my ears like I'm going to pass out, so I open the car door and… fall.

Onto concrete.

Splat!!! on my face.

And black out.

Ringo scrapes me off his driveway and tucks me into his spare bedroom—the one I 'fell for' Finn in.

In the morning my first thoughts are, as usual, of what I can serve my young VIP for breakfast. But something feels very wrong. My face is tight, like I've been covered in plaster of Paris as a joke.

Ringo explains what happened with the bedside manner of a master surgeon. I hobble to a mirror, seeing my upper lip's gashed open, a red slash above my nose, and my face swollen into eggplant parmesan.

I have to do what you can only do if you're hooked up to an IV drip—call in sick. Nick's tone is hostile until I say I fell in my bathroom and need stitches.

"Oh. No, you stay home. I've got it covered. The waitresses can count. Take a few days. Take a week."

"Thanks, Nick. I'm really sorry."

I can't go to the Medical Center because it will be clear that my injuries aren't from slipping in the shower. This looks like I faceplanted concrete. It'll get back to Mr. Malik that I've misbehaved in some degenerate illegal way.

So Ringo takes me downtown to Xamnesia Public Hospital. XPH is the lowest of the low. Only scant locals (not related to the VIPs) and Bangladeshi construction workers go to XPH for anything involving a needle and thread. A waitress who had to go there for an endometriosis operation that wasn't covered in her employment contract said she woke up with dried blood on her pillow. Somebody else's.

Ringo drives with great care in his Range Rover, as if I'm a grenade with its pin dangling out. I wait on a cracked orange bucket seat and Ringo brings me a can of diet Coke that he thoroughly wipes with his Jane's Addiction sweatshirt before I put it to my lips. My head pulses like a quasar, one of Ringo's baseball caps half-hides my smashed pumpkin face. It's a souvenir from the SEAL concert. I think back to how SEAL chatted up Charlotte during that concert. Those were the days.

A doctor—I guess that's his qualification—finally sees me. The X-ray machine is greasy with grime, but no bone's broken. He butterfly stitches between my eyes and tugs six stitches through my upper lip as tears roll.

Because of my strange 'shower slip,' I'm given seven days off. I hightail it to London to see Idora. We squeeze in a side trip to Paris where we get tipsy in a Greek restaurant in the Latin Quarter, smashing plates and picking up two guys, who drive us breakneck speed around the Arc de Triomphe to some nightclub where we dance till closing time. The next day we wander around Montmartre and walk along the Seine with the two guys, who are both 'in love' with us and whom we revile.

Idora is the voice of sanity when she drops me at Heathrow to return to Xamnesia. She's quitting to work on opening her dance studio.

"Why don't you quit, doll, move here? You have a British passport, you lucky duck."

"Yeah, or India? Or I was thinking of moving to

Vancouver and working in film. I have a friend there who's got a job in a production company…"

Idora looks sad for me. "A lot of options."

My VIP calls me over.

"What happened to your face, Lizzie?"

"It's when I slipped in my bathroom, Sir. Sorry…"

He frowns, maybe sensing I'm lying, maybe thinking, 'What a klutz' or maybe looking straight at me for the first time and thinking, 'Something's not right with this picture.'

He behaves impeccably on his diet. While my stitches disintegrate. Finn and I get back 'together.' I have been on this yo-yo on-and-off rollercoaster before with the five-year relationship back in Auckland, but I am oblivious. I am so happy that Finn wants to be with me. Of course I go back.

24

MEN 5

I count another 240,000 calories and devise another 480 meals. 370 days. I am Calorie Counter for 370 days when I write my letter of resignation and leave Xamnesia on August 5, 1998.

Mr. Malik says on the phone from Paris, "Your VIP trusted you. Motherfucker." His directionless motherfucker is forlorn.

"I'm just tired." I confess. Don't tell anyone you're tired.

Mr. Malik says a gruff, "Thank you, Lizzie. Keep in touch."

In the Sports Complex, my VIP stands up to say good-bye, with a 'thank you,' and shakes my hand. I feel like I'm letting his down so badly I almost recant.

The butler hands me an envelope. 30,000 *drachma*, the

usual. US$15,000. Seeing money doesn't give me a high or low anymore. It looks like rent, cigarettes and bottles of champagne, it looks like delaying having to make grown-up decisions. It looks like Xamnesia in action: a handy life-blurring fog of invincibility. Nothing can hurt me with these lovely red bills protecting me.

But inside the white box isn't a pretty diamond watch; it's a white, plastic-strapped G-Shock. A sports watch. Is my VIP that pissed at me for abandoning him? My last hours, I hide from sight again. I am wallpaper curling off a wall.

At 1:30 a.m. the butlers ring me, gibbering.

I am with Finn on the couch, watching *Total Recall 2* again, where heads block the screen on the badly pirated version, but we choose to 'see' around them.

"Miss Lizzie, where are you now?"

"He's up to 1,780," I reply wearily. "So just two baked samosa and three sticks of celery, and sliced pear if he's still hungry… Okay?"

"I give you the wrong white box," he babbles. "Where *are you*? I send driver."

The poor butler got it in the neck for giving me the wrong box. By 'white G watch' the VIP meant a white leather-strapped, opal-faced, diamond-encrusted, pretty Gerald Genta. Worth closer to US$5,000. Not a plastic white G-shock.

I pack up my pathetic life with nobody to witness the 'pack your suitcases confessions and tears.' What would I say anyway? Nothing.

I arrive back in Auckland, telling myself this is a holiday. I am *not* staying here. It is so full of gossip and friends half-owning each others' lives and experiences. One dear friend has been going through a divorce yet everyone seems to have taken it *personally* that the couple are no longer there, together, for them. Like, how dare they? Didn't they twig that their apartment was the social ground zero? (A contributing factor to the marriage breaking up…)

The ex-boyfriend moved in with the woman he dated directly after me. I can't move for bumping into some guy I fancied or got messy with.

Finn's phone call is a bolt of lightning.

"Angel. I miss you. I love you. Please can't you give us another chance?"

Why, yes. Yes I can. Because I love him and I'll do anything, even move back to Xamnesia for no job just for *love*.

You read that right. I move back to Xamnesia. I spend precisely three weeks in Auckland before hauling my Samsonites to the airport once again. August 31, 1998 I return to Xamnesia.

This is a moment when having three passports comes in handy. I use a whole new passport the second time I live in Xamnesia. My British one. The New Zealand passport was tattooed extensively with employment visas, private jet travel stamps, whereas my UK travel document is virginal and immigration gives me a one month's tourist visa without blinking an eye.

I move into Finn's strange bungalow and get all domestic. We acquire two kittens: Otter and Onion. Ginger tabby real twins, brother and sister who wash each other and curl up with us at night. Finn's work stress melts off of my shoulders. He's so stressed he wakes up in the middle of the night to smoke. I continue to not eat much, mainly curries I make. I have no car, which means no car crashes, but also no independence. And I have my novel to finish. I sit there, air-conditioning on, coffee at my elbow, ashtray slowly filling, writing and writing and writing.

It's not *exactly* the village I imagined I'd sit in to write after working in Xamnesia.

We pop over the border to the bars there for fun. We drive drunk in Finn's Kijang. We fly to an island with a big tourism industry and go scuba diving. Yes, I didn't mention that I trained for scuba diving. Because I didn't. The diving school is so Mickey Mouse that they let us dive eighteen meters (sixty feet), after a mere ten minutes of instruction.

When I'm down there, eighteen meters deep, everything is cloudy. I 'know' my contact lenses are safe behind my mask and I feel the heavy oxygen tanks feeding me air. But then I lose sight of Finn and the diving instructor.

I start to panic and shoot toward the surface... but the instructor appears out of the murk, grabs my hands, and keeps me in one spot. He looks me in the eyes, *Stay still. You will be okay.*

Slowly, slowly, he helps me ascend, his hand in mine. Taking three minutes instead of my panicked attempt to surface in thirty seconds. Finn pops up five minutes later.

"D'you see the sea turtles, angels?"

No, I did not see sea turtles. I did not see shit. I panicked and tried to give myself decompression illness by shooting to the surface like an idiot.

I shake my head, nobody sees the tears coursing down my face.

That night, by the hotel poolside, I get a little drunk and tell Finn that the key VIP isn't such a nice guy and what happened that evening, but Finn gives me a look, like he suspected it all along. And I merely feel tainted and worse for sharing. The key VIP's image never comes off dulled or tarnished. He is the messiah to his desert rats. *That was your fault*, is the look I receive.

A few Sundays later, Finn gives our babies, Otter and Onion, away to a neighbor—because he has an extremely paranoid weekend imagining that on Monday he'll lose his job and he believes the cats need a more stable home than ours.

That night we have our first full-on argument. I'm so mad he gave away our babies. It's like he gave up on *us*. After my Thai friend told me that Otter is *such* a lucky color of orange. I can't believe this *shit*.

"How could you give them away?"

"Look, angel. It's no use. I'm in love with Marianne. I always will be. That's the truth."

Marianne's the married woman he had an affair with back in Australia before even coming to Xamnesia. Of course, she's been in the background of the whole 'relationship' or 'flirtation' or 'fuck-buddyness' that we've had for six months. I pick up the phone and call Xamnesia Airlines for a flight to London the next morning.

He drives me to the airport.

"We can't say we both didn't try," he says, pulling me into a hug.

I land at London Heathrow at dawn on November 3, 1998.

25

MOVEMENT 5

London that winter of 1998-1999 is the usual freezing rain and darkness by 3:40 p.m.; plus the unusual panic attacks when I lie down to sleep.

I submit my novel to literary agents and a petite, energetic woman signs me on as her client. She has a bigtime Booker-Prize-winning author in her stable plus people like myself, who could be the next Booker Prize winner, she enthuses. Mr. 20 Percent Compound Interest reports that I'm doing *very well for myself* with my principle now at US$81,000: up twenty-thousand dollars. Of course I keep it all invested with him and go out temping. At first I work at Café Rouge in Soho then I get a desk job as personal assistant at the BBC. My pay is around £365 per week. I stay at my parents' flat in north London. They are busy with Jocelyn again in hospital. 'Overmedicated,' Mom says.

My new boss is somewhat moody. She compulsively chews pencil ends, speaks in a way that only a psychic can follow about code-named projects, flings her arms around like a hurdy-gurdy to communicate, speaks to the development team as if they're idiots, plays the politics extremely well with the other producers, demands I go buy her an Americano every hour, and collect her ridiculous amounts of dry-cleaning. My gay colleague dubs her SINBAD: 'Single Income, No Boyfriend, And Desperate'—but I like her. Her screaming fits are white noise compared to Mr. Malik's blowouts.

I try to fit into this new Lizzie who takes the 38 bus, then the Central line tube to reach work, who earns a measly £18,000 per annum but has weekends off, who dates a variety of nationalities but finds them all to be so weird I never progress to the second date (at least I'm not succumbing to any disastrous love affairs). I hang out with some of Jacqui's friends from when she lived in London, but the friends I get closest to are obsessed with sourcing cocaine every time we go out. I try the occasional line and find it's exactly the worst thing for someone like myself: transforming me into an expansive, confident bubble of Lizzie. A bubble that pops by daybreak. But so many people in London are on it, on it, on it. It's Charlie this and naughty-salt that. I seem to attract that kind of friend. The party people.

Jacqui's ex-boyfriend, Tony tries to line me up with a job for another VIP. An exiled one who is way well off and likes to travel to Geneva and just needs a travel companion. I agree to meet up with 'HRH Aziz' for a pseudo interview. At Annabelle's restaurant in Mayfair.

He's a huge lumpy walrus full of self-doubt with a high-pitched giggle.

I can barely keep up disinterested polite conversation and make it clear halfway through the main course that I'm not interested in the job with him.

"I'll drop you to your tube station, jump in," he offers outside Annabelle's after our meal which cost who-knows-what because my menu had no prices. It's freezing and raining so I hop into Aziz's black cab, leaning forward to ask the driver to drop me at Green Park Station.

As soon as the black doors click shut, Aziz's tongue launches down my throat. I push him off and yank at the door handle to open it. The driver pulls over on Curzon Street.

"You're a foul jerk!" I yell into Aziz's face, spraying outraged spittle but livid with him, with *men* like him (and you can guess all the men on that list by now).

I walk in the rain to my tube station and crawl into the flat, soaked and disgusted. I ring up Jacqui's ex, Tony.

"Thanks for the set-up with that lech."

"Oh what a shame, Liz! My friend who worked for him sued him for sexual harassment. I figured you could do the same, no?"

"No, Tony."

I stay in touch with Justine. This is what leads me to working in Paris. The job at the BBC was going fine. It was my inherent queasiness about all things England since being stuck in Brighton for months nursing a foul-mouthed sister. And the weather definitely gets me down. Paris always seems lighter than London, even if it's just as rainy.

I go see Justine for a weekend and she offers me my old job back, but in Paris. I say, "Oui!"

26

INVISIBILITY 4

Jumping back into working for the Xamnesians, why did I do it? Whenever you're offered something, there are the pros and cons. To this list you must always add *yourself*. Are *you the con?* I was a major negative point in any equation at this time. There I was, twenty-six years old with US$81,000 in the bank. Possessing talent (I could take care of others, no sweat) and intelligence (you never saw such an organized worker) yet utterly lacking in confidence and self-esteem. I still scrabbled in thin air. Was I always like this? Shy and curled in on myself, only gregarious with the aid of champagne? Uneasy in her own company? Oh yes.

Maybe this inherent Xamnesian way of thinking—the don't-mind-me-I'm-not-good-enough-anyway state of mind—*was since birth?*

Before I get all Freudian on myself, I haven't told you how I had a false twin, then another false twin, then no twin when I was born.

How you ask, how does *that* happen?

Good question. Like everything that went askew in my life, I believed it was my fault because I didn't breastfeed *right*.

I was a gigantic baby—nine pounds two ounces padded with fat and sporting abundant black hair—"Like an Eskimo," Mom used to say before that term became politically incorrect. I didn't cry when I emerged, I lay there, blinking at the fuzzy blobs, as you've read. Let me tell you what happened next, dear reader.

"What is it, is there something wrong with the baby?" Mom jabbered into the silence.

"No, Mrs. Harwood, she's just taking a look around," Dr. Doyle replied. Dr. Jack Doyle encouraged Mom to have us last three kids. She named Jacqui after him. And my Dad's dad had just died, ten days' prior. I guess Dad was there when I was born, but I doubt he was really *there*, having just lost his own father.

They did the usual APGAR tests to be sure I was a-okay. Somebody made me cry for that and I got 9/10. At five minutes of age I already wanted to keep Mom happy with a high level of achievement.

So, breastfeeding commenced and I have to add that my mother was a *professional* breastfeeder. She was the local leader of *La Leche League*, helped countless local mothers get the hang of it and breastfed all of us kids (except for my big brother Billy, our adopted sibling who started life in an incubator for two months). Mom was *au fait* with what to do.

But I wasn't. I was screwing it up.

I only fed off one breast.

Why? I don't know. Clearly I was an ornery little pain in the behind. The one-sided feeding threw Mom off-kilter, you could say, and as she lay in the daffodil-yellow maternity ward, chatting with all the young mothers of Rotorua that week, she noticed a pale redhead in the corner who turned away when the nurses came at her with her newborn.

Rhona's mother.

She was sixteen and giving up Rhona for adoption. She couldn't look at her child. The nurses had to bottle feed this little baby, so Mom, with one breast exploding with milk just going to waste, lived up to her Scottish heritage of *waste not, want not* and offered to breastfeed Rhona.

Ah, it was love at first sight.

I'm not saying my mother didn't love me, but boy oh boy, the way she describes Rhona, she was pathologically in love with that baby: tufts of red hair, perfectly shaped mouth, fed like a trooper, never a whimper, not even gassy. Meanwhile, sourpuss Liz steadfastly refused to go over to the other breast, even when Mom tried to slip me half asleep across the Mason-Dixon Line and sneak that nipple into my drowsy mouth, I'd jerk awake with a pissed-off squawk. *What are you doing, Ma, trying to kill me?* Rhona and Mom bonded. Completely.

While I only bonded with... half of Mom.

Rhona's mother remained resolute about adopting out her baby so Mom filled in the paperwork on day three to officially transform her into a Harwood.

When my parents adopted my brother Billy, there had been no problems. And it looked like the same deal now. Mom's adoption application was approved. We could soon go home. Rhona and Liz. Adorable false twins.

That same evening, the paternal grandmother swooped in from Auckland and contested the adoption. She left with Rhona (and there ended Rhona's breast-feeding).

Mom was crushed.

Crushed and full of love hormones.

The maternity nurses, seeing Mom slip into grief, suggested this whole other baby who needed adopting. A boy. Mom shrugged, said she'd take a look. He was a strapping baby, built like a future All Black, blond and hungry with a red face. So my parents adopted him, gave him a name, and *we* went home as false twins: Richard and Liz.

(Named, you might notice, for Richard Burton and Elizabeth Taylor who were still on their first marriage and making headlines with every move they made. The Burton-Taylors also adopted a child—maybe that was why my parents picked the name Richard because otherwise this is the equivalent of naming your twins Brad and Angie, which is a little weird, no?)

At home, baby Richard was a little… louder than any other Harwood newborn. He was hungry. He kept everyone up and demanded feeds around the clock. In short, he was being a regular newborn.

After ten days, Mom returned Richard.

When she tells the story, she implies that the older kids

weren't all that impressed and somehow pushed her to return Richard. But I know Mom. If she'd wanted Richard, she would've kept him. Trouble was, Mom had fallen in love with Rhona... not, Richard.

"A lovely family on a farm adopted him," Mom says, dismissing Richard in eight neat words. "But I never saw Rhona again... I used to peek into prams around Auckland every time we were there..."

I felt really bad for Mom when she talked about desperately seeking Rhona for months, even a year or two later. But I felt worse for Richard. Then I felt only horror at the casualness of it all. And guilt that me rejecting one breast somehow escalated into this false twin mess.

Ultimately, I think Mom was glad to have given those two the *breastmilk* because she believes that stuff makes kids more intelligent and have better immune systems...

I'm guessing neither Rhona nor Richard know they were Harwoods for a few hours or days. It's not the kind of story you would tell your granddaughter/adopted son —that you were sucked into this crazy family for a spell before landing in your true home. That you were breastfed by a mother of six who thought she was invincible enough to take on another baby, then a different one, then neither.

I heard this story when I was about twenty because it involved breastfeeding (me and my one-sided nonsense that kicked this whole debacle off...) and as breastfeeding is distantly related to the facts of life, Mom never breathed a word of any of this until I was an adult.

I imagine myself as a newborn in this adoption circus:

having one baby beside me, then a different one, then none. Shy and curled in on myself. Uneasy in my own company. Trying to do things *right* because I naturally fumbled. I needed time to get the hang of things. To be okay with who I was—fat, black-haired 'Eskimo' Liz.

27

MOVEMENT 6

"Everyone asks about you," Justine drops. "I think you're the only person who's ever quit that they miss."

That's what pricks up my ears. Being missed. Thinking I did a stellar job and that they appreciated it. And my bank account. I'm on less than £18,000 per annum (pre-tax) and London is so expensive.

Justine has a way of planting kernels of sweet-smelling potential way before she voices a thing.

"Can you come back? And run Paris? Please, Lizzie. You're the only one I can trust. I need to leave."

Run Paris. Now that's somewhere. That isn't rotting in the desert with corrupt nepotism left and right, I'm being offered the City of Light.

"Where are you going?"

Her bottom lip trembles, "I have to leave."

It's sort of a non-answer. But this I understand. I'm doing her a favor. She needs to quit. I need to be a good friend to her and help her leave.

Besides, this time I'll do it differently. I won't lose the plot and crash cars and faceplant concrete and debase myself with a commitmentphobe with a drinking problem. I'll be sure of myself. I'll *be* myself. I'll have support.

The fact that I speak only ten words of French doesn't faze me. I am ridiculously grateful to Justine for thinking of me like this. Paris! Again, I'm after the material security and to avoid making grown-up decisions such as forging a career. Yet, who wouldn't take a job offer like that in Paris? Would you? Who wouldn't say to themselves, *I can handle it.*

"Just say the word. Everyone misses you, Lizzie."

I say the word. It's so easy to slip into 'don't talk about anything' mode. On the Eurostar trip over, the guy on my left asks me all sorts of interested questions. I am a clam. This feels safe. It feels good to know I'll be protected and simply work, work, work. No more will I have to deal with the real world. Phew.

Idora and I spent my last night in London sitting up talking. Her studio is a slow grind, she's not sure it'll be a success. She's dating a guy who is insanely jealous of her speaking to anyone. "Are you sure it's the right thing, going back, doll?"

"You don't think I should?"

"No, I'm sure it'll be fab. It's just… the way Justine goes about these things."

What Idora can't say is that she hoped that we'd cope

brilliantly out in the real world after Xamnesia, which made us tentative and looking for safety nets everywhere—Charlotte has flitted to Tokyo and Moscow now with increasingly surreal relationship stories—and now I'm stepping back into the bubble.

"My agent's selling my book," I argue. "I'm making peanuts at the BBC. It's just for a year. To really set myself up."

"Yeah, yeah," she agrees finally. "You're right, of course, make some more cash. It's a good idea."

"What else can I do for my novel? It's in the agent's hands."

"Yeah, doll. Absolutely."

There was so much else I could've done for my novel. I just didn't want to bank on myself. I banked on the Xamnesians.

"Well, who wouldn't want to go live in Paris?" Mom says over the phone. My ninety-four-year-old grandmother has breast cancer and survived the double masetomy, but insists on a private room in her nursing home, which Mom and Dad can't afford. Burke (my ex-brother-in-law) died aphixiating on his vomit the day he was supposed to go watch my niece perform in a play. Mom's concerned about my niece. Jocelyn had another mini-breakdown, but hey! Good news! She got remarried. To a schizophrenic guy.

"You might as well get a bit more out of the fat cats.

Keep your savings tied up or else your siblings will only ask you for loans."

My life in Paris starts on the stroke of midnight May 9, 1999. If someone pulled me aside in Gare du Nord to tell me that precisely four years from today, I'll marry the love of my life, I would shake my head, *Not me, not Lizzie. True love happens for others, not me. I'm destined to suffer, buddy. I'm Wednesday's child. Go talk to my sister, Jacqui, if you want to see true love.*

But, oh, I'm here for what I do best! I'm determined to do the best job *ever*. I'm going to save my entire salary. I'm going to quit smoking and go to the gym. I'm going to start working on my next novel in my spare time. I'm going to learn French in five minutes.

It's the usual to-do list of the desperate, ping-ponging around life.

The key VIP is in self-imposed exile, darting between Paris, London, and New York because some major crap went down in Xamnesia. His people revolted and banished the whole lot of VIPs. Everyone is concerned for the tribe. How will they cope being unable to return to home? They need their most loyal staff. Can you see me waving my hand? That's me! Miss Loyal!

The driver, an older black man called Etienne with a 'Mlle. Lizzie' namecard, nervously places my Samsonites in the back of the Renault Espace and drives with trepidation as if I'm a VIP who will sever his head if I am displeased. How bizarre. The streets shine with drizzle—no scorching heat or deluges here!—and pretty neon advertises life happening on every corner. 'Tabac.' 'Hippopotamus.' Everything looks and sounds alive, welcoming, easy. Taxis abound. I can walk on these sidewalks. Paris is beautiful. He pulls up at an address on rue Faubourg Saint Honoré, the back entrance to the VIP's property. The seven-foot, bulletproof steel door has no keyhole, only one solitary buzzer on the videophone. If the security guard inside the Control Room doesn't recognize your face, the bulletproof door doesn't open. I will never hold keys to where I live.

The driver carries my two Samsonites across the threshold then darts off, saying in broken English he's not allowed inside the residence.

A Goliath approaches. With craggy eyebrows and bright eyes, shock of black hair, near-Albino pallor, and a curly white communications coil poking out of his ear, he looks half-Terminator, half-Frankenstein.

"I'm Ray. It's good to meet you. Let me take those," he escorts me up in a huge, stainless-steel elevator. Back-of-house gives me déjà-vu: cold gray tiles, no elaboration, all business. I shiver.

Ray shows me to my bedroom and… have I made it clear that it's a garret inside the VIP's property and thus I can never have anyone over for a cup of tea, let alone to stay with me? A window allows in light but doesn't open. A kitchenette out in the landing is shared with other members of staff, including nannies. Nannies. I am filled with dread.

"Can't I rent my own place? This is like living in a prison. With the nannies."

Ray winces, "Yeah, I know it's inside their property. You could rent your own place… sure, but you can't say who your employers are. I guess there are agencies that would rent to you no questions asked, but that would cost an arm and a leg."

"Let me give it a try," I give him my college-try smile. I don't want to spend all of my salary on rent. That wasn't the point of coming to Paris for this job. The point was to save, save, save. To be careful with my money. To set myself up. Not break the golden egg and get yolk all over myself.

Ray seems like a nice guy.

Justine appears, with big hugs.

She immediately drags me out to a bar, Hôtel Costes, to be precise. The bar at Costes doesn't close, or for me it doesn't ever seem to. Justine lights cigarette after cigarette over a perpetually-topped-up flute. I eat all the tiny black olives and almonds while she warns me of many things of upmost importance.

"Back in Xamnesia they've turned the key VIP into a scapegoat because of the coup. If he didn't have the lawyers he has he'd be in prison, or even dead. The conservative factions there want him hung out to dry."

I think of how maids were sacked for hanging their underwear out to dry on their balconies, and of the mythical rope we were all given to hang ourselves with. I edge back in the plush pink armchair with golden tassels and gulp another mouthful of Veuve.

Things have calmed way down—he no longer needs red birds' nests in Naya water bottles set out in the sauna, he hasn't bought a hotel in a year, and the list of entourage has quartered. But how can the family maintain themselves if they're cut off from their oil?

I, however, am mainly thinking, I did it! I landed on my feet in Paris!! This is fucking fantastic.

I barely take in what Justine is saying. And it's bewildering to *speak*, not scribble our words down on pads of paper to be incinerated afterwards on the balcony and watch the ashes float skyward.

"Maybe we can go over everything tomorrow?"

But, this is my handover. Gossiping in Costes until two-thirty in the morning over two bottles of Veuve and two bowls of olives and slivered almonds.

I stir in my bed, stretching my limbs and checking my watch: 10:03 a.m. Shoot—I slept in.

My cell phone erupts in the obnoxious Nokia ringtone: da-da-naa-naa-da-da-naa-naa-da-da-naa-naa-naa as I step out of the shower. The sound makes my skin crawl.

I could tell you all the ins and outs of my day, but, again, I'd have to kill you. Suffice it to say I did the usual fifteen-hour days. I slept badly due to phone calls at anytime o'clock. Pretty soon I knew every nut and bolt on the Eiffel Tower, every sales assistant on rue Faubourg Saint Honoré and avenue Montaigne, every toy in Toys'R'Us, and everything on Ladurée's menu. But did I need to speak French? Not really. Most sales assistants saw the ripple of green in my bulging petty cash wallet of 500-Franc notes and suddenly spoke their best English. And I had my secret weapon, the concierges at a certain five-star hotel owned by the key VIP. I had them on speed dial and recognized if it were Bertrand, Pierre, Jean-Charles or Hugo at the sound of their '*Bonsoir, Conciergerie.*' I had Paris in my back pocket.

After each bout of VIPs hanging out, loneliness hit town. I knew nobody and my paranoia coated me like the wrong shade of foundation. I'd go to WH Smith, to a book event, but the second my phone blared I ran out onto rue Cambon. I never took the *métro* because my cell phone signal would dry up. I walked or cabbed everywhere. I invited friends and family over and put them up at a four-star hotel nearby. That was cheaper than finding an apartment at three times the normal cost.

And every time I spend petty cash on items required by the VIPs, Marie Curie smiles up from every green swirly note as if to forgive me for not using this cash to cure cancer or vaccinate poverty-stricken children. I feel a little sick at how many 500-Franc bills go through my hands. At EuroDisney. The Lido. Cartier's. Galeries Lafayette. The women's eyes widen at each checkout or sales counter. I smile in apology and wish I could explain to them, *This isn't me. This is just for a year.* I find myself spending a sizeable chunk of my salary. On the friends and family who visit. On things I need to feel better. On cigarettes and champagne. But not on a gym membership. What if my phone rang while I was underground somewhere on a treadmill? I'd get into trouble.

I'm in a Renault Espace with Michel the driver. My head spins trying to follow his running commentary. As we rumble over the Champs-Elysées's cobblestones, all I grasp is that all these nice, wide boulevards were created so tanks could roll in and crush the serving classes.

My agent rings with the latest round of enthusiastic 'I'll pass' responses to my novel.

"What do you suggest I do?" I ask her as we swing around the Arc de Triomphe. Being in a car in Paris freaks me out considerably. I cannot imagine *ever* driving a car in France.

"I'm chasing up Serpent's Tail, Orion, and Fourth Estate, all who've had it for ages."

"So this is normal? I don't need to rewrite it?"

"Take it all with the habitual pinch of salt!" she enthuses and I hope she doesn't mean 'naughty salt' like everyone seems to take in great pinches in London these days.

I hang up the phone, confused. What's happening? I got a writing grant, I wrote my novel, I got an agent, how can it not sell?

But then my Nokia blares again and I forget my writing 'career' with the next urgent VIP request.

28

MEN 6

Outside the back door, I light up a cigarette, waving hello to the Versace sales assistants, blinking in the sun's glare after the dim frankincensed, cologned, interior of the residence.

I walk the six blocks down to Cartier's, asking for Samira, the glamorous Lebanese woman, and hand her $29,000 for a pink Pasha diamond-studded watch for somebody's birthday.

I peek inside the Envelope that lurks in my handbag. It is US$10,000. I can tell myself that the Envelope is an extra thank you because managing Paris is such high maintenance, having to be visible so much in front of the VIPs and go out with everyone on all outings. But it's probably his thank you for what just happened on the carpet of his Study. Which changes the meaning of the money. You can guess what just happened on his carpet, by the way. Go ahead, one guess. Duration of the event:

five minutes. Duration of how long I will judge and beat myself up about it? Years.

Benjamin Franklin, who adorns each one-hundred-dollar bill gives me a repellent glare, "*What were you thinking?*"

"Butt out. It's my life," I stare back.

"*Just how low is your self-esteem, Liz?*"

"*Shove it, Ben.*"

Meanwhile, Samira in Cartier makes small talk, asking if she can take me to lunch next week and whether I speak French.

"I don't speak French. But, lunch would be nice, I guess."

I wonder if she wants to be my friend. Most likely she wants gossip and for me to ask her you every time I come in to buy things the VIPs want. She must be on commission. I watch her smooth hands with beautifully-shaped nails, slip the diamond item into the red-on-white Cartier box, wrapping it snug with a wide, bright red ribbon. She looks like she takes care of herself.

Why did I lie down on the carpet? I don't know. But I am determined not to do *that* again. Was it to feel a little bit special? To feel like I can't screw up and get fired? To give me a cloak of invincibility against the palpable politics surrounding the entourage around here? To mimic what Justine had—that oozing confidence that I am desirable?

This is so horrifying, these thoughts running through my head that I jump up, thank Samira for the diamond item, and run out onto rue de la Paix.

When each visit ends, I emerge, blinking, from the fifteen-hour days and constant rushing. But I really *don't* speak French. I know nobody in Paris. I can't go hang out with Bertrand the Concierge, can I? My closest 'friends' are the Hôtel Bristol valet guys. That's not a pack. I can't talk about what I do. I'm *too cagey* to make friends. I pay for language classes and join writing groups, but then another visit is announced and I'm fifteen meters underwater for the next ten days, missing classes. So I drop out. Look who's the commitmentphobe now.

Paris isn't the easiest place to slot into for a paranoid property manager who lives in an inner city fortress with a bunch of security guards, a scary-looking Frankenstein guy, and a couple of Thai maids, who doesn't know what to do with herself on a day off because I'm exhausted and the VIP now rings me to see how I am doing. Every day. *Just like Justine*, I remind myself. *You are falling down a rabbit hole.* But what can I do? Hang up on him when he calls? I literally run out of hair salons with my head covered in foils when he calls. I look like Medusa on the street. I meet new people, but constantly compare their world to my Xamnesian cotton-wool wonderland and the real world is in black-and-white, while his is a Technicolor insider's joke.

I figure there's only one way to skirt around the carpet. Get a boyfriend. When the VIP says, "Keep it for me," I think he'd be put off *it* being spread around town.

The trouble with that is, ever since Manu's bleating

causing Charlotte to crash her car, I have a physical aversion to French guys.

In the summer of 1999, as the potential book deal dries up completely and a solar eclipse happens one morning, I'm run off my feet with Madame in town, the female VIP who merrily sacked Laundry staff because of the wrong underwear arriving at her property.

Madame's personal assistant, Wilhemina, takes over my office. I find Wilhemina on the office PC, her perky black bob shaking with mirth over whatever latest e-mail joke she received (people are e-mailing now! I even do it!), strews of receipts around her, chewing her Guarana gum, doing her bit to rack up the thousand-dollar phone bills around here.

"Ah, Miss Lizzie, you are finally UP!" she crows.

It's 10:00 a.m. I've been up for an hour, thank you, Wilhemina, but have to make my calls from my garret since she's down here and we're not supposed to talk about anything in front of Madame's staff.

"How are you? Everything okay?"

"Okay Dokay," she pushes a pill bottle my way. "Miss Lizzie, can you, with all your knowledge of this wondrous city of Paarrrrriiiisss, buy this for Madame? She say you can try, too."

The label reads Xenedrine. Three large pink pills rattle inside. "What's it for?" I ask.

"It marvelous. Diet pill. You can eat all you want and whoosh, everything just leave your boddddayyyy."

"I'm not sure I want that."

"Go on, Miss Lizzie. Madame say you can try, so you try. She will need as many bottle as you can get for us. Thank you."

I could phone our contact at the American Hospital, who makes house calls for a mere US$1000 per visit, but figure I'll try the pharmacy first. Often medicine is available without prescriptions. Or, it is for me, anyway. I walk to my druggist off the Champs-Elysées and she sells me a dozen bottles without a shrug.

Wilhelmina's in raptures when I produce the Xenedrine so easily and pushes a handful of pills my way again.

"Honest, Miss Lizzie, you try. It's marvelous."

So I do.

Photos of me in 1999 are—in all honesty—stunning. I'm slim without looking like a cadaver as I did when I stopped eating, I'm full of life with a beautiful smile. Of course I look great. I'm so *young*! Twenty-six and living in Paris, remember? I don't need diet pills. I take them to please Madame VIP though. Overly adaptable personality strikes again.

That afternoon Madame and the kids hit EuroDisney. It's a sticky one. The kids are fractious. Even skipping the queues with the Guides takes too long. I'm reconsidering how much to tip these amateurs when it takes ten minutes to get on Peter Pan's Flight (cutting a ninety-minute wait for normal people).

"Lizzie, what can we *eat* here?" Madame asks, her voice like fingernails on a chalkboard.

The Guides shepherd us into a roped-off area of the fast-food café inside the Pirates boat ride where it's mercifully as cool as a cave—like the caves I imagine those red and white birds' nests are harvested.

"*Fi*nally," Madame sinks into a plastic bucket seat. Her two human fans flap faster.

I kind of over-order, as I tend to do when obtaining food for the VIPs plus their entourage. It's easier to grab twenty of everything, hose everyone down with Coca-Cola and diet Coke, and shrapnel all with fries. I end up eating chicken nuggets, hamburger and a large fries, plus slurping a Coca-Cola. So much for diet pills spiriting away the appetite.

After lunch we lurch into Adventureland and by the time we reach the Haunted House, I'm in serious pain. If I don't cross my legs and clench, I'm scared I'll crap my underpants.

"Y'all right, Lizzie?" Simon, the kids' bodyguard asks as the elevator descends and the walls stretch twenty feet tall. I have backed against a wall, as far from the family as I can be, a junkie's sweat pearling my forehead.

"Yeah, fine, thanks, Si," I smile, clenching every muscle in my lower body.

Not only am I in danger of explosive diarrhea, but my heart's beating the foxtrot—do I need an ambulance?

What I don't know is that the 1999 version of Xenedrine took whatever fats you swallow and turn them into yellow bile to excrete, so while your body got used to this fantastic news, any doctor would tell you to avoid fried foods or your bowels would go ape. But I took the pills on Wilhelmina's medical advice.

I tiptoe around the haunted house, slinking into the last carriage with Korean newlyweds to be spirited around the possessed dining table of ghouls—my eyes water in concentration to prevent any *pfffft*s loose.

Working for the family means you can't walk off mid-anything, even if you need that IV drip. I clench and perspire for a further two hours until, at last, Madame says she's had enough of all these people and we clamber into cars and burn up the A4.

I lean my forehead against the cool rectangle of glass as stone suburbs slip by.

But it isn't over.

"Lizzie?" Wilhelmina rings from Madame's Mercedes. "Madame feels like a sandwich before we return to the house, where shall we go?"

At 6:00 p.m. in Paris, mid-August—tourist month—when precious few cafés had heard of continuous service…. My mind goes blank.

"We'll have to try Costes I guess… not many places serve food all day… but dinner service only starts at, maybe seven…" I pant.

"Madame wants her sandwich *now*. Not at seven. I tell driver. You ring other drivers. We try your Cos-tes. Thank you, Miss Lizzie."

So I drag twenty-odd bodies, the majority being butch nannies in white smocks, into the most chic, snooty spot in Paris and try to convey that these are important VIP people (with their butch nannies). And for once, my best friend Costes doesn't play ball. Nothing is available to eat. I know that if Jennifer Aniston walked in with twenty lepers, they'd be served anything. But Madame gets nothing. I beg, eyes pleading, buttocks jellified, but nada. No sandwich.

"I'm so sorry, Madame, it must be because it's August…"

"Never mind, Lizzie. Not your fault," her growl conveys the exact opposite. We convey to deposit her at the Front Door.

I bow outside the Front Door as she marches inside, then I hobble around to the staff entrance, up to my garret toilet, where I erupt like Mount Vesuvius. I may have learned my lesson on dieting. But not on beating myself up for getting things wrong, or doing every last thing requested by the VIPs.

29

MISCHIEF 4

When the key VIP isn't in Paris, I go everywhere else: London, Rome, New York for a weekend or whatever amount of time I can get Mr. Malik to okay. Or I ask friends to come over and who wouldn't agree to that? I buy company.

If I'm stuck in Paris with nobody around, I eat *carottes rapées* (I assume they're grated, not raped) that I buy at the *8 à Huit* grocer's off rue Faubourg Saint Honoré. Or I eat dinner alone in Café Castiglione. If it sounds like I'm asking you to get the big violin out, yes, sure, I'm being the biggest blockhead and should just be falling in love with the city, discovering Paris inch by glorious inch. But, truthfully? Paris scares me. I don't hang out at the markets and buy amazing food to cook. My kitchenette has an oven in it but it's never been turned on. I'm bone tired. Plus, let me tell you what happens when I venture out to discover Paris inch by glorious inch.

One Sunday, I go see *The Ninth Gate* at the Gaumont

on the Champs-Elysées. Except I go to the 10:15 p.m. screening. Mistake number one. The film's two minutes in when I realize five seats along, the man is masturbating. There is so few of us in the audience that it must be provoked by the sight of me, or Johnny Depp. I am frozen with the sound of his wet *schlock-schlock-schlock* that speeds up until he grunts.

A minute later he jumps up, grins in my direction, wipes his hand on the theater seat, and leaves.

He probably followed me into the screening. I start hyperventilating. It's like 'Harvey' again. I leave twenty minutes later, praying he isn't outside.

I walk down the Champs-Elysées, shaky, lighting a cigarette, rainy drizzling, feeling low and stupid and exactly how I felt in Auckland before I left. Paris makes me feel unsafe. I go to the wrong areas at the wrong times of day. I hate hanging out here by myself.

Worse, next time the VIP rings, I tell him. He is outraged, a tickled-pink outrage, a getting-off-on-it outrage.

"Really? He did that? How can you be sure?"

I describe it. This is stupid stuff I'm doing. I get all manner of sympathy from the key VIP. It's letting my guard down by telling him what upset me.

After that, I insist on taking the security guards or Thai maids to the movies with me. But after movies like *Fight Club* I have to talk them through it scene-by-scene afterwards. I can't explain to their satisfaction why Edward Norton has to shoot himself in the head. I sure know why he does.

I sit in the darkened room of the Drouot auction house trying to follow the prices things sell for. One of the female VIPs wanted free of her dresses, stilettos, and never-worn La Perla sets—it isn't to make money—nothing sells for anything like the price she paid. I imagine her years of shopping to accumulate this colossal waste.

"You buy something," Ray, who came along, urges.

I raise my hand for a pair of black Manolo Blahnik boots. They're size seven; I'm a five, so I plan on giving them to Idora. Nobody else bids so I get them for the retainer: 400 Francs. Fifty dollars. I laugh into Ray's freakishly giant shoulder.

In fact, the Manolo Blahnik's fit. They are so pointy at the toes that size seven is more like a five. So I keep them. They are beautiful. I bought them for someone else, not me, but it turns out, they are meant for me. I inadvertently do something nice for myself.

I stand in the private dining room of La Tour d'Argent—the duck place. This celebrated restaurant has served heads of state, film stars, the French elite, and rich tourists since 1582 when French royalty gave them a starred review. It is famous for its *caneton* and the wine list is 15,000 options thick. The restaurant fell from three Michelin stars to two in 1996, but this hadn't dampened the public's taste for bloody duck (*canard au sang*). It's our kind of place—the soup costs $60 a bowl and an entrée of caviar is a mere $220.

The maître'd, a sinewy man with a beak nose, goes over the details. In daylight the view is gorgeous, at night it will be a twinkling dream—the panorama includes the hooded-eyed back of Notre Dame, the islands, and the silken shimmer of the Seine dotted with tourist monofoils swaying. Monsieur Cheverny is the picture of cooperation: how the table should look, what flowers won't provoke anyone's hayfever, the lack of wine and no mention of such a *haram* liquid for these good Muslims, no Cointreau in the dessert, changing the fish course to vegetarian for one of the entourage who hates prawns, ensuring no beef slips onto the Hindu entourage's plate. But in double-checking that our pressed duck will be *halal*, Monsieur Cheverny is no longer my pal.

"Madame Li*tz*ie," he draws himself up to his full six foot two, "it's not possible."

No way will Claude Terrail, the octogenarian owner, bring in halal-slaughtered duck to squish in his special press. Their duck are pre-strangled on their farm. I'm duck out of luck.

"But it's impossible for Muslims to eat non-halal meat. We can pay extra, of course, for the inconvenience. Someone has to pray over the duck—before cutting the jugular, can I find someone to do it?"

"It is not a matter of convenience. It is a matter of tradition. We do not pray over the duck."

I return to the residence in a panic. Fucking duck.

Unhelpful French. I'm positive this would never happen in London or New York—civilized places where restaurants can be paid to come to an understanding, places where 'customer service' is alive and well. Only here would tradition overrule money. What they do to their poor ducks is already sick, in my thinking: strangling them, pressing the carcasses to collect blood, cooking them in a sauce of their own blood and bone marrow! Somebody *should* pray over their poor animals with that post-mortem barbarity. I'm a voice of reason, here.

Dinner is scheduled for Friday, too, the holiest day of the week. The VIP already told his guests we're going there. I'm dead in the water.

I linger out back, smoking, waving a distraught hello to the Versace sales assistants, unable to muster small talk with our loitering drivers. Mr. Malik hops out of a taxi after visiting the Hindu temple near Montmartre.

"Why sad?" he demands.

I quietly explain the halal duck disaster.

"What can I do?"

"Come, come," he ushers me up to his suite where a waitress appears with coffee and *pain au chocolat*. He commences whacking one fist into his palm, cackling, "You tell them the motherfucking bloody duck is 100 percent halal. If a Muslim doesn't know the meat *isn't* halal, then they don't go to hell for eating it."

"There's a halal loophole?"

"Yes, yes," he twirls a hand. "*You* burn in motherfucking hell for all eternity, but they go to heaven with the virgins." He laughs his head off.

So I put my neck through the halal loophole and beam at the sprightly eighty-year-old traditionalist Claude Terrail, lead the group upstairs past framed photos of famous faces who ate this sacrilegious duck (the postcard count is in the 700,000s), to our kidney-shaped table with the million-dollar views.

I pronounce the pressed bloody duck to be halal. And make damn sure the waiters who understand English do not negate me, or they can forget their tip.

I slap down payment for dinner a little brusquely—Marie Curie face down—and only tip 10 percent, since La Tour d'Argent consigned me to hell after this life. If I believe in that sort of thing. Do I?

I find a woman called Jane who lives in Montparnasse and teaches meditation. I ask her to hypnotize me to help me quit smoking. I don't feel hypnotized though. I feel very, very conscious of her voice. I don't let myself go under, in case I let my Xamnesia façade slip and accidentally tell someone the truth about everything I try to forget in my life.

30

INVISIBILITY 5

It's December, 1999. Fears about the Y2K bug don't concern us, but fears about money do. The cashflow's frozen and staff hasn't been paid for two months. I have nothing in the Société Générale accounts here to pay my stack of monthly invoices for the residence.

I walk over to rue de la Paix to Cartier's. The air outside is suspended and dull, despite the gay wreathes of green and twinkling white fairy lights. This millennium will be finished in a fortnight. I have a rotten feeling in my stomach a lot these days, like I've surpassed my own best-before date.

Samira approaches to kiss me on both cheeks and we both smoke as we contemplate the diamond-studded purchase.

"You look a little tired. You must be busy."

I set down the cash, "Really? I slept like a baby."

"However did you end up in Paris, my dear?" she presses.

I revert to my Funny Girl façade that marks me to these Parisiennes as distinctly foreign—open and chatty, but I'm saying nothing. I feel like someone wrote 'Irredeemable Slut' on my forehead in lemon juice ink that appears if you apply heat. But Funny Girl won't let anyone close to her with anything such as warmth.

"I'm from a family of seven kids," I reply. "We were encouraged to go in any direction we fancied… free as birds. So I ended up here."

"Really? I'm one of seven, too," she snaps the large padded white and red box shut. These red on white boxes make my stomach churn. "But nobody's really 'free as birds,' are they?" Samira muses. "We're part of the society we live in, the culture we grew up in, our families—even if we left them behind."

She's saying I have a blank canvasness to me that I really shouldn't have, which floors me for a moment. She's right, we are supposed to be tied to our homelands, to the countries and cultures that mold us into adults. Why have I erased myself? I have to face the reality: I am *not* being myself here in round two of working for the Xamnesians.

If I were on the *Titanic* I'd be one of the stupid violin players. Jacqui would get herself in a lifeboat. Idora and Charlotte would be fished out of the frozen water before any harm occurred. But I'd be rearranging deckchairs and darting below decks to check how high the water level is, telling everyone not to worry about me.

I jump on the 7:11 p.m. Eurostar to London Waterloo International on December 15, 1999, for a mini-break.

Mom is in London, plus my eighteen-year-old niece, Kina, who I adore. Jocelyn's kid. I'll also catch up with my brother and his wife and kids. I want to buy some new underwear and as usual, my hair needs doing. The Paris coiffeurs do what they want with my locks. Idora listened more in the desert.

I hit London, cab to drop my stuff at mom and dad's council flat in Islington, promising to spend proper time together the next day and by midnight I'm in a flat in W1 drinking champagne with friends of friends and taking detours to the upstairs bedroom for a few lines. As I said, I normally avoid coke, I'm too scared of what I might promise people under its chatty influence, but my head's off in the clouds tonight and I'm taking a few risks. Trying to fit in with the other twenty-something-year-olds with disposable income in London. After line three I'm a chirpy girl. I *like myself.* I stop the self-judgment for two seconds. But I'm about to jump into another mess.

The VIP phones with his usual, "Hello, Lizzie, can you hear me?" doubling my heartrate. I look at my Jaegar Le Coultre: 1:15am. He never rings so late.

Why can't he leave me alone? Doesn't he know this is my three days off?

"Hello, Sir," I lock myself in a quiet bathroom, and sound sleepy.

"Lizzie!" Madame interrupts. "You are in London! So am I! I just hear this! What are you doing here?"

"It's time off, Madame, a couple of days. To see my mom."

"You must come over."

"Come over?"

"Yes, come and have a drink. Trey will collect you."

I say, "Okay, Madame," and promise to go the next evening. I hang up and go find another line. Thinking, they'll either forget all about it, or if Trey's there (he's their DJ) that'll be okay. I guess it's sweet to be invited. As if I am worthy of actual conversation, as an equal, almost.

Trey rings, at midday, to get my address. I don't want to go. I feel wretched.

"I thought they were joking."

"Sir just rang to remind me to remind you. They're looking forward to it."

"So you go see them for drinks often? This is normal for London?"

"Yes," he's ticked off. "She told you that. The driver will collect you at 11:00."

The assignation weighs me down, as does my rattling head, the drip-drip-drip down the back of my throat, the itchy shittiness. I'm grumpy with my niece, Kina, and, when my sister calls, I tell her to quit with the constant message-relays. "If Queen Elizabeth II's really murdering 600,000 girls then ring the police," I snap. I escape with my niece to Upper Street to try and shop. But niece's help doesn't work—I'm in too unstable a mood to buy a thing.

We return carrying take-out. At nine o'clock I mention that I have to go into work later, for a while. My mom frowns sharply and Kina gives me an incredulous look.

I put on work clothes: navy trousers and a pink Ralph Lauren cotton shirt with a blazer. Hang my little pink Louis Vuitton handbag over a thick cream overcoat.

"A driver will bring me back. I've got my key."

As a child of a schizophrenic who won't take her medicine, this niece, Kina, has seen more than her fair share of delusions. She gives me an incredibly sad look from the saggy beige couch.

"We'll go shopping properly tomorrow, promise," I wave.

The driver picks me up. It's freezing.

I see Mom's silhouette in the kitchen window, watching me go, or looking for her fox—who lives in the backyard and she faithfully feeds with porridge and chicken skin daily.

Walter the driver complains the whole way about how many hours he works these days, dropping me at the back entrance to a cream three-story mansion in Mayfair.

I don't want to go into too much detail of what happens inside the mansion. It's no doubt obvious to you, dear reader, why these Xamnesians would invite Lizzie over at midnight.

By one-thirty, I've downed way too much vodka in order to please them, danced the cha-cha and lost at cards, lost my clothes as the other three people lost their clothes…

I know I should jump up and leave at the realization that we are gambling with clothes. But, instead I clutch my fan of cards and focus on the rules of the game. The rules are so simple, I'm sure I won't lose a stitch. And, just like back in Auckland, I don't feel *that drunk*. I am numb to the world and in a state of blind invincibility. I am Xamnesia personified.

If I hear that song, 'A Little Bit of Sandra's What I Need' I feel those hideous hours in the mansion all over again. That is the song I cha-cha-cha'ed to. Trey the DJ replayed it a dozen times. It sounds so innocuous, the male singer just *needs* a variety of women for different functions. *This is me*, I think as I drunkenly fall onto the couch. This is what I've become. One name of many, to entertain. But when Madame sticks her tongue in my mouth and her talon-like fingers slither around my clitoris, everything snaps and I start screaming my head off.

The key VIP and Madame disappear.

Trey shouts at me to *shut up* and pushes my clothes at me.

He bustles me out into the freezing night air into the waiting car, and then I remember nothing else.

31

CRASH 3

This should be the part of the story where I have an epiphany, the clouds part, a rainbow-streaked unicorn of love shows up, and I turn it all around.

Not yet. Not the next morning in mom's two-bedroom flat with grime around the toilet as I throw up, panting, retching until my eyes stream with tears.

Later.

I haven't even returned to that day in March, 2000 when I'm smuggling the million dollars for these guys. Remember that? Feels like such a long time ago.

My epiphany shows up in another year and a half, at the opposite end of the world, in Thornleigh, twenty miles outside Sydney, Australia.

Today, I'm too sick to float up into the sky, float home

to my 38,000-foot high haven, and have the perspective to forgive and heal.

Today I'm in denial. I'm in the land of it's-my-fault-but-I'm-fine. I don't tell Mom what I've gotten myself into with my dream job in Paris for the generous, rich ones.

When I reemerge, Mom rails: "I've never seen anyone so close to an alcohol-induced coma. I'm suing that smug fat cat that you slave for."

It's somewhat comforting that Mom wants to wage war on my behalf, but A) we both know we aren't suing anyone, and B) there is an anger to it: *how could you let yourself get in that state?*

I react as if Mom's mad at another kid. I pull my bathrobe tighter around my wrecked body and ease onto the saggy couch. This isn't happening. I am the 'sorted out kid.' I can't face Mom's disappointment in me, it makes me want to die.

Kina the niece eyeballs me.

"It's fine. I'm fine."

Kina gives me her most spooky perceptive look. I always try to be a role model for my nieces, an auntie who is a success through hard work and going for life's exciting opportunities, and look at the unraveling—worse, the *disemboweling*—of that little fantasy.

I go throw up again, but have nothing to give the toilet.

There is nothing to be done, I figure. Trey would never testify on my behalf. The driver only saw a drunk member of staff in his backseat. Nothing *really* bad happened.

It's better to be Miss Amnesia.

"What were they doing to you anyway? What do you have to do over in Paris for them?" Mom follows me into the bathroom, annoyed.

"Nothing. It's just because I was here on holiday."

"You need to quit, Liz. What are they doing to you?"

"I didn't eat enough yesterday."

And, Mom believes me. She's always believed me. 'No, I didn't go to the pub.' 'No, I wouldn't drive Dad's Triumph drunk.' 'You don't have to worry about me, Mom.'

I retch again.

There's nowhere to go to from last night. It doesn't enter my mind for even a second to go talk to the police or a lawyer.

I went there of my own accord. I should have stood up at the sight of the first vodka. I screamed and stopped it in time. I can't stand the thought of making last night public knowledge. I'd die of shame. *Envelope Number 15 Please Sir.* It's my fault for not seeing it coming.

I truly see this as my bad. Justine never had any female VIP jump her. Idora's never been propositioned. Charlotte neither. Kristal was never invited over for tea, let alone an orgy. It's because I am worth less than them. I'm the one who takes such little care of herself that it wouldn't bother me. I am the one who'll do anything to keep others happy. I wear tatty underwear.

I choke on the tap water my niece hands me in this

grubby-walled, calcified faucet, cotton-curtained flat. I come from this. I come from Harwood stock who get suckered in and wiped-the-mat-with and what's the best we come up with? Humor. Remember Culloden. They'll slaughter us, but let's go down with self-deprecation.

I lean back against the sink stand. This toilet needs cleaning. This shower is encrusted with soap. I see every bottle of bath bubbles I've given my mother. She's never opened or enjoyed a centimeter of them. Not one bath rose unfurled. Everything is saved for that rainy day.

"You should quit if they're not nice to you," Kina offers. She is totally right. I brush it off.

"It's nothing, really. Forget it."

I understand the key VIP. He doesn't like to let go. He waits to see a crack in people that he can get his fingernail under and lift open.

But I can't explain this.

You're fine. Don't lose the plot.

Don't tell anyone anything.

I know even if I tell Mom everything right now—an act requiring a breakdown on my part—what can she do anyway? Once she faces the disappointing, crippling, fatal (to her or me, probably it's me) fact that even her most 'together' child is a mess, she'll have to give me some sort of an answer, right?

I return to the lounge and turn on the TV.

Mom leans out the kitchen window, throwing leftover porridge to her fox mommy and kits.

My phone rings.

"Hi, Lizzie. How are you?" It's Trey. Overly chipper and casual.

"Bad."

"Sir isn't happy, he tried to call, but you let someone else answer your phone."

Don't let someone else answer your phone. Amendment: unless the VIPs put you into a near coma.

"That was my niece. My mom almost took me to the hospital."

"Well... you remember about tonight, though, right?"

"No." This has to be a joke.

"You promised to come to dinner. A proper, sit-down dinner. Nine o'clock."

"Trey, there's no way. I'm sick. I am on the bathroom floor. No. Tell them I'm *in* hospital."

"I can't! He already phoned me today, he won't phone again."

"Get a message to Madame. Call Wilhelmina and tell her to tell Madame. I'm not going. I'm not doing it."

"No. I'll send the driver at 8:15. You'll be fine by then."

"I'm not going."

"You have to, they're expecting you. It's arranged. It's too late."

I crawl into bed and fall asleep.

At 8:15 p.m., I wake to Walter ringing; he's outside, waiting. Mom is freaking in the lounge, "What's that car outside for, Liz? Have they come to harm you?"

I brush my teeth. I insert my contact lenses. I ask

Kina if I can borrow some clothes since I don't have anything clean left.

Of her teenager's wardrobe strewn across the carpet, I pick out unwashed jeans, a striped polyester skivvy, and red sleeveless bomber jacket from a charity shop. I push her Converse onto my feet. Cinderella ready for the ball.

"I won't be late," I tell her. "Believe me."

She eyeballs me. I've run out of 'belief' credit.

Walter is taken aback. I never wear jeans to work (since Whitney Houston's concert). Nobody wears jeans to work. And these jeans carry a scent of incense and marijuana. Walter remains silent all the way to the property as if I am a walking contagion. I slip in the service kitchen door.

Trey stands, gripping kitchen counters (clearly feeling like crap), checking food as it slides into silver chafing dishes. He's in a tuxedo, his hair all on end, like a penguin who had a cardiac and was reanimated with electric paddles.

"*What are you wearing?*" he's as white as a sheet. "It's black tie."

I bite my lip. His disgust hits with nuclear force. I am supposed to feel shame here but right now I feel impervious.

"You forced me to turn up. Here I am."

Sweat breaks out on his forehead.

"Come on," he drags me by the arm into the foyer. "They'll be here any minute."

The roar of the VIP's car is heard and Trey opens the double doors.

Him: tuxedo, waxed shoes. Her: red Dior haute couture, a blindingly massive diamond choker, four-inch heels, fit for the red carpet. Me: grubby jeans, skivvy, bomber jacket, unwashed hair, nails no way manicured, after puking all day.

Trey babbles, "Lizzie's really sorry, she didn't remember what we all said about making a real effort and dressing up for tonight, she didn't feel very well this morning, and she didn't make it out shopping in time…"

"Trey said he couldn't cancel."

They recover in seconds. It's suddenly no problem. Trey pours Dom Pérignon. "No, thank you," I put my hand over my flute. Nobody drinks.

Dinner is over quick. I am a total joykill.

Next time in Paris, when the key VIP circles his desk to approach me in the Study, I step back with my hands raised.

"I have a boyfriend."

"Oh?" His eyebrows shoot skyward.

I don't have a boyfriend. It's a positive visualization. If I say I have one, I might manifest one into my life, as Jane's meditation lessons encourage.

He busies himself in moving back behind his desk.

"Lizzie," he looks up, a glint in his eye. "Can you talk to Angela for me?"

"Talk to Angela?" One of the not-so-attractive female bodyguards.

"See if… she'd like to come see me here, one morning…"

"She wouldn't," I reply.

"Oh?"

"No, Sir. She would run and tell Madame."

"Just the Cartier watch, then. You can do that for me?"

"Yes, Sir."

"Thank you, Lizzie."

For Christmas and New Year's Eve I take another mini break. I go see Jacqui, who's happy in Sydney, Australia, with Eric, her fiancé. She's five months pregnant. She's only two years older than me, but streaks ahead of me in this game. Engaged. Baby. Buying an apartment. I don't see myself as capable or worthy of marriage and kids, maybe ever. The thought of being a mother freaks me out. Our little brother, Sam, flies down from Canada. It's a reunion, of half of us kids, at least. It took Mr. Malik so long to approve this time off that the only flight I can get leaves on Christmas Day and arrives December twenty-sixth. Bertrand and the Concierges can only find me a Business Class fare. What a different Christmas Day this one is compared to four years ago, after our brush with 'Harvey.' I fall sick during the flight—it's the Millennium Bug that everyone's been getting.

I go out with Sam for New Year's—Jacqui's now sick with the bug I brought—*How could you, Liz?*—when she's pregnant and everything. We end up in the Casino where Sam wins $840 at Black Jack by betting on number twenty-three, his number, as the sun rises on January 1, 2000 and no Y2K bugs eat up the world.

I'd like to ask my little brother if he has a gambling problem, just as he'd probably like to ask me about some of my problems, but instead we spend a lot of time outside Jacqui's building, smoking sneaky cigarettes, soaking up the Sydney sunshine. It's like being a kid again, there's no problem that can't be fixed by movement and our little crutches.

32

MEN 7

It's cold in Gare du Nord as I wheel the million dollars toward the customs agent with his drug-sniffing, muzzled Alsatian.

I volunteer to take over this money because after shutting down the body shop, I kept open my loyalty boutique. By spurning the key VIP's advances, I feel like I have to say 'yes' to pretty much anything else.

And there's another reason why I would never run away with this money. As of January 2000, I do have a boyfriend, Rik. Rik's not the kind of guy I'd tell that I'm carrying a million dollars for my VIP bosses today. He's Dutch ex-police, now a bar manager. How he went from police detective to bartender is a story. He ate some chicken, apparently, and ended up in hospital for three months, lost all of his muscles and was dropped off the force.

It's not an option to run off with a million dollars because Rik would find me before the Xamnesians ever would, even at the bottom of the Black Sea, and he'd want to do *all sorts* of things with this sort of money. He's already asked me to loan him US$20,000, which I did without batting an eyelid. He got into terrible debt in Amsterdam after losing his police job and I like to feel useful, remember? In some way, it's like I found my fake twin, Richard, after all this time, working in a bar in Amsterdam, looking fragile after losing tons of weight from eating bad chicken.

All the friends who have met Rik so far approve utterly. He dotes on me, dolling out affection and *really* listens, while pouring the Veuve Clicquot at Titanic Bar and Grill in London, or Costes here in Paris, or The Supper Club in Amsterdam. I move in this Bermuda Triangle of Paris-London-Amsterdam. It's exciting and I'm happy.

Dropping this million dollar bundle in London is a cinch and I'll be able to catch up with Idora tonight, before heading back to Paris tomorrow. Rik's due in on the Thalys tomorrow at 10:00 p.m.

The customs agent barely glances at me. The dog doesn't stir an inch. In fact, he gives me a look of—what is it?—acceptance: *Wow, that's some guts you got, look at you. You go, girl.*

I ignore the German Shepherd's weird look and take a seat beside the Haagen-Dazs stand, light my millionth cigarette, propping my feet up on the Samsonite.

Onboard my train I put the suitcase at the end of the carriage and keep it in full view for the whole trip. The image of the Samsonite etches onto my memory.

I am planning my departure from Xamnesia.

Rik and I are talking about moving to Sydney. Opening a bar. As my novel failed to sell, maybe I'm not a writer after all.

When I quit, in September 2000, after as many months of my US$10,000-per-month salary as I can stomach, Rik and I do move to Sydney. We're going to open that bar. Rik has been traveling (on my tab, of course) to Miami and Singapore to scope out bars and get all of the ideas. I am fronting up money; he's the fount of creativity.

The other reason I quit and move to Sydney is that Rik kept pushing me to get *him* a job with the Xamnesians and I can't do that.

"Go on, Lizzie, get them to invite us both over for midnight drinks. They'll like me. I promise."

"No, Rik. No. Way."

He's quite unhappy about my attitude. He even punches the bedroom wall beside my head in his four-star hotel room one time to express this unhappiness. But I want to be out and far away.

A friend from Auckland, who moved to Paris with hopes of making a life there teaching English, takes over my job. I worry about what she'll encounter, but she's sliding into debt and can't get enough teaching hours to stay here. And she wants to stay so badly. It seems like I'm a mean friend if I don't give her the job.

I spend a lot of time on the handover, so she won't feel at a loss for information.

I also say: "If you're ever approached by anyone with anything funny in mind... because I heard that happened to a few female employees... don't feel pressured to do anything."

"Of course!" she says.

On the flight down to Sydney and our new life, Rik and I travel with Jacqui and her five-month-old baby. Another beautiful niece I'd like to see grow into a confident girl with no shaky sense of self.

Rik has a meltdown in Bangkok, trying to upgrade himself into business away from my sister, baby, and I for the second leg. His meltdown turns onto me when Thai Airlines won't comply. In the Smoking Room, he shouts, *"You fucked it up for me! It's your fault, how could you do this to me?"* I feel my world tilt, it's the fatigue from not sleeping on long distance flights, it's the rush of nicotine to my brain, but it's also an inner tilt.

I look at Rik's angry hands as he cracks his knuckles and think, "This is the stupidest thing I've done yet."

33

VISIBILITY 1

In Sydney, my former roommate, fellow 'Harvey' survivor, Jessica, greets us with Dutch tulips to welcome Rik.

It's October, 2000, springtime in the southern hemisphere. I rent us a sunny apartment in Pyrmont, the area Jacqui lives in. I open a bank account, dump months' of salary in it to live off. I don't buy a car (afraid of accidents) and try to live like a normal person. I am already somewhat fearful of how much money the bar will require. I'm thinking a cozy little hole-in-the-wall place. Rik is envisioning The Supper Club (a huge bar/restaurant where patrons are served on massive, all-white beds).

Things unravel. With Rik, it's a simmering wake-up to how unstable he is. It hits me when we fly from Australia over to New Zealand for Christmas, 2000, and he belittles me in front of my school buddies. (He also takes to pushing me around physically during our increasingly frequent arguments.) We are in Auckland when I tell him I need to break up.

Ugliness ensues. He sits outside my oldest sister's home in Ponsonby all night on Christmas Eve, cajoling me to take him back. It's all my fault. For bringing him to the other end of the world. I am *responsible* for him. My big sister is brilliant, repeating all night, "You're doing the right thing."

I drive him to Auckland Airport and tell him I want him gone from my apartment by the time I get back. I'm not scared of what he'll take from the apartment because with everything I've given him already what else is left? I've bought him professional DJ turntables, a thousand-dollar telescope, the clothes on his back, and the suitcase he can pack it all into.

When I return to Sydney, I ask Jacqui's fiancé, Eric, to help kick him out of the apartment because he's still sitting there in angry denial. It's a horrible scene. I feel so guilty for destroying Rik's dream. I change the locks the second he leaves.

For the next three months, he stalks and intimidates me, living in an apartment within fifty feet (the police can't do anything other than give me an emergency support number). He hacks into my e-mail account and pretends he worked for the Xamnesian VIPs in job interviews (Sydney is almost as small as Auckland so this news gets back to me through a friend of a friend's). Every night I lie in bed and pray he will get a job far, far away from here and leave me alone.

Jacqui's wedding happens. I'm fraught and on edge with Rik around the corner. My black-belt-in-karate big brother offers to go punch Rik in the head. I almost say yes. But there is a bigger family hurdle looming. Jacqui's odd symptoms since her car accident in 1993 manifest into a diagnosis of multiple schlerosis. Jacqui, the beautiful beach-pretty brave and sharp-tongued, has an incurable auto-immune disease on the brink of her wedding. You can imagine the messes we are at her hen's party.

After Jacqui's gorgeous nupitals (complete with the baby niece tugging at the front of my backless dress so much that it hangs all askew and everyone sees my tits when I lean forward to sign as witness), I realize I need a little help.

My former roommate, Helen, always talked about this guru-type guy, Mike. Mike happens to live in Thornleigh, outside Sydney, and counsels people like me who have lost the plot.

I travel up and down to Thornleigh for months of 2001 to talk to Mike. It's an hour by suburban train each way. At first I think it's a colossal waste of time, but I soon understand how chronic my programming is. My panic attacks and state of Xamnesia—wishing for invisibility and rash self-destructive behavior—isn't going to peel off me like a bad sunburn. It's layers deep.

I hear news from Mr. 20 Percent Compound Interest (hey, remember him? I was up to US$100,000 when I last heard from him). It takes him one split second to lose all of my savings in the dot-com stock meltdown. I plunge into depression, knowing that Rik will never pay me back a single dollar of his 'loan.' But hey, at least Rik left Sydney for a job in Tokyo.

I take myself off to India for a few weeks, with Charlotte, where we talk a lot about life and funny things that happen to us and how it's really best not to dwell on the negatives and only imagine the best, brightest, lightest things for ourselves.

It takes me most of 2001 to scratch the surface of rewiring my negative thinking. When Jacqui reports that both Eric and our brother Billy say I make lousy choices in men, at first I slump and want to jump off the nearest roof, but Mike's cognitive-based techniques helps immensely: *I prefer not to make lousy choices in men, but if I do, it's okay and I'm not going to die.* I visualize and cross my hands over each other and imagine blowing out flames of anger that rise inside me for being so stupid and full of shame. I have to repeat it an awful lot: *It's okay and I'm not going to die.* At all times of the day and night, this wave swamps me and I begin to remember.

I remember the things I put down in this book and with every wave of feeling stupid, naïve, weak, worthless, erased or invisible, I stay with it, retrace my steps, and rewrite. *I prefer not to feel stupid/weak/worthless/erased/invisible, but if I do it's okay and I'm not going to die.* I stay with all of it: the car accidents and ripped off toenail, the smashed face and rash behavior with guys, the heavy drinking, the starving myself, the acquiescing for the key VIP, the letting Madame gamble for clothes and pour big drinks and jump on me, the retreat from my family and shutting out friends when I felt judged, all my sad, faulty attempts at love that I've botched and messed up because I never loved myself... *I prefer to be liked/loved by everyone at all costs, but if I am not then it's okay and I'm not going to die.* I ask my heart, *How can I manage this better?* And I repeat after Mike: *I'm a blessed child of the Universe and the Universe is taking care of me.*

Of course, all this is difficult to explain to people. It's best not to, in fact. It's best to do my little visualizations, blowing out flames of anger and fear, and mantra stuff off in a corner away from onlookers who may question my mental health. Between Jacqui and Jessica, I have a few onlookers who are very ready to jump in with well-meaning advice.

When Jacqui is huffy at me for putting my problems onto her or phoning at the wrong time and waking up the baby, or when Mom repeatedly asks, "Well what about your book—when is it being published?" and "Has Mr. 20 Percent given you back your money?" and then, "Can't you do something about it?" and "What were you thinking, Liz?" Then Mike advises to laugh to 'announce the game' and tell them, "I love the way you're trying to protect me but I am a big girl now," and to myself I add a whole dance routine of hand-crossing, flame-blowing, and *I am not going to dies*.

Hey, we Harwoods weren't brought up as any particular religion. I quite like my conversion to a child of the Universe receiving unconditional love. This is better than running like wild boar on the bush tracks of the Barrier and never telling our parents what we were up to.

That year I also write a bad second novel about a

young woman who goes on a Ferris Wheel in Paris and spins into a parallel universe where she has this whole different (better) life, but really she's just a nutty cow and has been cheating on her boyfriend... Yeah, it's bad. Clever for the sake of being clever. *Aie, aie, aie,* as the French would say.

My savings goes from US$100,000 to *negative* US$3,000. As September 2001 approaches and my twenty-ninth birthday looms, (*the* age, Jacqui's husband Eric says, when women go into overdrive to secure a man to marry), I am almost exactly where I was at twenty-three when I jumped for that job in Xamnesia, chasing material security to escape Auckland and student debt, so I can go live in a village and write. It is five years after receiving the Envelope full of Cash and I have almost maxxed out my credit card, with no assets to my name.

I have one asset, homework from Mike: a Vision Board, an A3-size collage depicting the beautiful end result I choose for myself in the areas of love and self-confidence, which I look at every day and tell myself will happen.

I have no plan for my life. I fly one-way out of Sydney on September 5, 2001.

34

LOVE 1

I leave Sydney, heading one-way to London. All I have is my collage with cutout photos from magazines depicting a beautiful romance, and a Me who exudes confidence. Admittedly, a lot of the pictures are from perfume adverts and there are probably a few too many images of champagne bottles, but I like looking at it. *I prefer to find a man who isn't the guy off the black-and-white Eternity fragrance ad, but an actual, living guy, but if I don't find him, I am not going to die.*

En route to London, I stopover in Bali—for Charlotte's wedding to an amazing guy, along with Idora (who's just moved in with her own amazing guy). The wedding is in the paddy fields of Lombok and is utterly perfect.

I stay in Bali until after my birthday—we all go out to dinner to celebrate—and I see Idora off at Denpasar Airport. She's flying the opposite direction, down to Auckland to see her family. When I give her a hug goodbye, something catches in my throat and I start to cry—I don't know why, but my tears roll and roll. When I return to the bungalow, Charlotte, the other wedding guests, and I see black flames choke the TV screen and the Twin Towers' unbelievable fall happens before our eyes.

I arrive in London on September 15, 2001 and Mom's at their apartment. She's cut all her hair short again. Recently, when she was looking out the kitchen window for her fox, she saw a man stabbed to death by another man who was paranoid-schizophrenic and released from a mental health hospital too early. The schizophrenic man then went home and tried to kill his mother but instead killed himself. Mom had to describe everything to police, she told them about the blood and how it pooled in the dead-end cul-de-sac.

One afternoon, I decide I need to be brave. She just boiled the kettle. I make us each a cheese sandwich with Piccalilli. Mom's been heckling, just a little, to find out what I'm going to do about Mr 20 Percent losing all my money, and adding a nice guilt-trip: "Why couldn't you stay in Sydney where Jacqui needs some family around her and somebody to help her?" and "What are you going to do now?" She's right. I shouldn't be sitting here sponging off her hospitality. White sunshine streams into the kitchen and I watch Mom's hands cross over smoothing down the padded tea cozy and marvel at how good her skin looks and how much like a young girl she still is at seventy.

I open my mouth and all these black, slimy eels fly out in a speaking-in-tongues projectile. I tell her *some* of what happened in Xamnesia and Paris working for those VIPs. That I pretended I was fine but I wasn't. That I smoke like a chimney and drink too much for a girl. Don't eat proper meals. That it was Jacqui who crashed our cousin's car, not me. How I drank underage in pubs and bars. Drove Dad's Triumph absolutely blind.

My mother's not equipped to hear a solitary thing about promiscuity, drinking alcohol or power spells of the excessively wealthy.

She pales, but clings to her arguments, "How did all that happen? And what about Justine? She was so pretty. I liked her."

"Well, she certainly was pretty."

"And your friends, Idora and Charlotte?" she continues.

"No," I sigh because she's turning this into the others, not me, when I'm trying so hard to talk about me, for once, "nothing bad happened to them. Apart from general paranoia and brainwashing."

"Well? What's the difference between them and you?"

"I'm *me*."

She frowns. I've lost her. She doesn't know what I mean when I say that.

"Kiddo," she jollies. "But you were the one I never had to worry about. You were always singing and dancing, a big smile on your face. You were always so *happy*."

"Maybe I needed just one minute of worry."

"Look, kiddo," she grips my hand with her bony, hot

fingers. Mom always has such warm, warm hands. "I knew they were all rotten, those people you worked for. But I'll fix them."

"It's okay now, Mom."

"I'll put them on my List."

"Your what?"

"Of bad people who've done wrong to my kids. That rotten boyfriend of yours, Rik, is on it. And Mr. 20 Percent Bullshit. You'll see. That'll fix 'em."

"Okay, Mom. Thanks." I sip my tea, biting my lip. That's what she's got to get through life? A List?

But is her List any different to my Vision Board or my hand crossing and flame blowing? *I'm okay and I'm not going to die.* Who am I kidding? *We* are *all going to die*!!!

I think back to one hypnosis session with Mike to help me quit smoking (which hasn't happened yet). I did go under. I went far under inky darkness and traveled out as if I were dead. But I wasn't dead and gone. I was in the dark night sky as a star. *We don't die*, it felt like something was saying, *we go into the inky sky and shine.*

Mom and I drink our tea. The beige saggy couch is so comfortable and the September sunshine fills the room until it hums. It's okay. I can get myself back by myself. I always suspected that I can't simply make Mom say what I want her to say just as she can't make me be perfect for her, *I prefer to be perfect for you Mom, but as I'm not, it's actually okay and neither you nor I have to die.*

"I love you, Mom."

"Me too, Liz."

So we go out, round to my brother's, to have croissants rolled up with cottage cheese inside, and stuffed grape leaves, and juice, and I go upstairs to sit in the nieces' various bedrooms and see that they're reading *Harry Potter* to each other and loving the act of reading, and I answer their questions and say I honestly don't know where I'm going now and that that's fine.

I also mention never trust guys who offer 20 percent compound interest without getting their father to check the contract. And make it a policy to tell *someone* in your life the truth, always. At least yourself and preferably yourself plus others who love you.

I go to Paris the following weekend—I promised my friend who took over my old job. She's turning thirty. At her birthday dinner at China Club near the Bastille, a French guy is invited, Mickaël. He knew the other Kiwi gal at the table from working together at Danone (chocolate cookies and desserts). He sits beside me and asks all lots of interested questions, which I try to answer with real answers (still not easy). We progress to a tiny bar called Wax and dance for so long that we start kissing. We kiss and when we surface it's 2:00 a.m., the DJ is shutting down. We are the last two people on the dance floor.

Mickaël looks like the photo I put on my Vision Board to represent Love: the guy with short dark hair from the black-and-white ad for Eternity hugging and kissing the blonde on a windswept beach.

I have met my beautiful end result.

35

POSTSCRIPT

This'll sound a bit mental, but I then work again for the Xamnesians, for a further two years. But it isn't to my detriment. It's a regular office job. I make a decent salary, which dropped to US$2,500 per month and I never saw another Envelope—working for Xamnesians must be the only job in the world where you actually earned *less* the longer you did it. I spend more than half on rent because I choose a short-term furnished apartment not too far from work, but it's plenty for me.

It's not the same experience as the previous two times. Third time works a charm, perhaps. I prefer to think that it's my perspective that changed the reality. In fact, in the end I am fired (or made redundant, it does mean the same thing) for not being respectful enough about the latest female VIP on an e-mail (not realizing that they bugged my e-mail). In the end they *do* give me just enough rope to hang myself. But who cares? It's just a job. It doesn't define me. I'm okay with myself and not so self-judgmental. I make mistakes but sometimes the end result is letting go of people who dragged me down. When you start seeing yourself as deserving and loved, then you can bid adieu to the drama and gossip.

My second novel doesn't sell either, and I part ways with my agent in London. I approach insolvency accountants and eventually receive US$20,000 back. Mister 20 Percent is still out there investing so watch out for him in bars buying you champagne.

'Eternity Guy' (Mickaël) and I's relationship is the easiest, nicest thing in the world and after nine months of dating I move into his apartment, and nine months later, on May 9, 2003, we marry. We return to being happy non-smokers on New Year's Day, 2004.

We marry in Paris, in secret. We mail little announcement cards to everyone, including our own parents. (Sorry to my mother-in-law, I know that was a shock.) We marry that way so that my family won't try to get there and some fail and it all be an uneven mess. So we have two other weddings—in New Zealand and Normandy—and the wedding in Auckland, on February 6, 2004, is the first time all of my brothers and sisters and nieces and nephews and our flighty parents are in one spot at the same time and space, fully present and accounted for, since 1990. An event that hasn't been repeated since.

Of course, Jocelyn speaks in riddles and is reduced to a stick figure; Kina's stoned and her dog runs off on heat so she never makes it to the reception; Sam misses half of the reception trying to get Kina to come along; my big brother can't attend the reception because the wine being served goes against his beliefs; and a day later Jacqui is in huff with our oldest sister, but we are all there for 100 minutes, at a ceremony outside in a park with Kauri trees shielding us and the air filled with rose petals and smiles.

We have the reception at Toto Restaurant, where Scottie changed so much with his rolling Rs and offer of Xamnesia. At the end of the night, a Latvian friend I worked with in Xamnesia has us sit on two chairs that the waiting staff throw into the air up, up, up as many times as possible to predict how long and happy our marriage will be. We manage to stay on our chairs, airbound, for many, many throws.

THE END

ACKNOWLEDGMENTS

This one's for Mickaël, who never suggested I give up this book even though it's taken me seven years and a lot of personal angst. It's not easy living with a writer and he handles it the way a bomb defuser would: suggesting I pick a wire and cut it, already.

If you're sitting there judging me as a self-absorbed, whiny, slutty cow then don't fret because I've judged myself with those adjectives and many worse. If you're sitting there thinking, *I feel like I've erased myself and live in a fog too sometimes, do I have Xamnesia?* then talk about it. You can even talk to me at lizzie@lizziehbooks.com. If you're sitting there thinking, *Look at you, you go, girl* then you are either a drug-sniffing Alsatian working Gare du Nord customs or you see this as what I intend it to be: a story about love and acceptance.

Thank you to author friends for reading multiple early drafts, and to PAGellas Kristin Duncombe, Samantha Vérant, and Jennie Goutet for final-hour editorial support.

I wish you love, dear reader. This one's also for *you*.

ABOUT THE AUTHOR

After years in Paris and Stockholm, I currently live in Auckland, New Zealand with my husband, children and rescued cat, Goldy.

Writers are nothing without readers. Please post your review on the site of your choosing. Even one or two sentences help enormously to spread the word. Thank you.

To get in touch, my author website is lizzieharwood.com you can also reach me at lizzie@lizzieharwood.com, Lizzie Harwood Books on Facebook, @lizziehbooks on Twitter and Instagram.

Join my mailing list http://eepurl.com/bkvg71 for new book releases and news.

www.ingramcontent.com/pod-product-compliance
Lightning Source LLC
Chambersburg PA
CBHW050857160426
43194CB00011B/2192